ADIRONDACK
NATURE NOTES

An Adirondack Almanac Sequel

ADIRONDACK NATURE NOTES

An Adirondack Almanac sequel

Tom Kalinowski

Illustrated by Sheri Amsel

ADIRONDACK NATURE NOTES
An Adirondack Almanac Sequel

Text Copyright 2010
by
Tom Kalinowski

Illustration Copyright 2010
by
Sheri Amsel

First Printing 2010

All Rights Reserved

ISBN-13 978-1-59531-034-7
ISBN-10 1-59531-034-7

Library of Congress Cataloging-in-Publication Data

Kalinowski, Tom, 1951-
  North country nature notes : an Adirondack almanac sequel / by Tom
Kalinowski.
     p. cm.
  ISBN 978-1-59531-034-7 (alk. paper)
  1. Natural history--New York (State)--Adirondack Mountains. 2. Sea-
sons--New York (State)--Adirondack Mountains. I. Title.
  QH105.N7K253 2010
  508.747'5--dc22
                                    2010030159

NORTH COUNTRY BOOKS
220 Lafayette Street
Utica, New York 13502

To my mom & dad
– T.K.

In loving memory of my mother-in-law,
Margaret Ackerman Prime,
one of the all time great Adirondack women.
– S.A.

TABLE OF CONTENTS

INTRODUCTION

The Adirondacks are a region of exceptional diversity. Climate zones shift significantly between the lowland valleys that lie along the edge of the Park and the highest peaks in the state; precipitation amounts vary substantially across the region; the soil, the water, in all its forms, the terrain itself all differ enormously across the six-million-acre Park. Even the impact of the people who have visited, lived, and earned their livings in the region over the last few centuries differs markedly from place to place. These and so many other factors have created a patchwork of uniquely special environmental settings.

As a direct result of this diversity, the flora and fauna of one location can be quite different from those of settings only short distances away. In my previous book, *Adirondack Almanac*, I focused on those plants and animals that are the most commonly observed around the towns and villages scattered throughout the Park. While *Adirondack Nature Notes*, too, presents the natural histories of some familiar creatures, such as the chickadee, crow, deerfly, and firefly, it also highlights forms of life that reside in places people only occasionally visit and rarely live and explains a few of the processes that occur in nature, such as hibernation and molting, that have a significant impact on the lives of numerous wildlife residents of the Park.

Adirondack Nature Notes is intended to be a broad overview of the inhabitants that exist in regions across the entire North Country. The stories of the plants and animals selected for inclusion in this publication illustrate the amazing diversity of life for which the Adirondacks are both famous and beloved.

T.K.

The Moose in Winter

The length and severity of the winter in the Adirondacks prevent many forms of life from existing in this region, yet these are two of the primary factors that have allowed the moose to successfully reestablish its presence in the northern portion of the Empire State.

The climate of any area is critical in determining the type of vegetation that flourishes there. The subarctic weather patterns that set the Adirondacks apart from the more temperate surrounding areas provide for the growth of plants that are better suited to the nutritional needs of the moose than any other hoofed mammal, including deer. Balsam fir and spruce, for example, which comprise a substantial portion of northern forests, bear needles that are readily ingested by this mammal and often become staple items in its diet. While the whitetail must confine its activities to lowland settings covered by these two trees during much of the winter, it does not have the ability to extract nutrients from either of these evergreens. The moose is also quite capable of deriving nourishment from the buds of the hardy species of deciduous trees and shrubs that are common in colder settings. Consequently, as winter becomes entrenched across northern New York, deer often experience a major problem finding the three to four pounds of browse per day they require to remain alive and healthy, while the moose has much less difficulty meeting its daily requirement of twenty to thirty pounds of needles and twig tips.

Not only is there adequate food for the moose in the North Country, it is food the hoofed mammal has the capability of accessing when there is a substantial amount of snow on the ground. The very long legs of the moose, which make it the tallest mammal in the Northeast, allow it to easily walk through several feet

1

of snow without becoming bogged down in the white powder. Additionally, a moose's legs move up and down, rather than swinging back and forth, further increasing its mobility in deep snow. While this high-stepping gait gives the moose an awkward appearance as it travels across a snowless landscape, it enables it to effectively maneuver in places with snow accumulations as great as four feet.

The bitter cold that frequently descends upon the region at this time of year is of no serious consequence to the moose either, as its exceptionally dense coat of fur provides adequate insulation from temperatures as low as minus forty degrees. Its large body mass also helps in conserving heat. (Smaller creatures have a greater surface area to body mass ratio that allows for a higher rate of heat transfer to the surroundings. This is why a small cup of hot water will cool faster than a much larger container at the same temperature.) The incredibly large mass of a moose allows for such a limited rate of heat loss that it is more likely to experience a problem with overheating during the summer than with hypothermia in winter. Air temperatures in the high eighties are considered to be the upper limit which this giant is able to tolerate.

The relatively low deer density in Adirondack wilderness settings is another factor that is favorable to the moose. In places in which the population of white-tails is high, an eyelash-sized nematode called brain worm frequently becomes widespread in the herd. While brain worm has very little affect on the health of a deer, it is fatal to moose. Conversely, in regions in which severe winter weather greatly limits the population of deer, brain worm also becomes scarce to non-existent, thereby allowing for a healthy moose herd.

The impact that winter weather has on the forms of life which exist in an area varies greatly. For the plants and animals that are best suited for survival in a temperate climate, our winters can literally become killers. For those forms of life that have evolved adaptations for a subarctic region, like the moose, the severity of this season is instrumental in ensuring that any encroachment into this area by forms of life more suited to a warmer climate is kept to a tolerable minimum.

The Muskrat's Winter Routine

Despite the covering of ice that exists on our many ponds and marshes, the muskrat continues to remain active throughout the winter in these shallow, weed-laden waterways.

Like the beaver, the muskrat has a permanent shelter in which it spends the vast majority of its time from late autumn until early spring. In most Adirondack marshes, particularly those that form in the backwaters of rivers, the shallow bays of lakes, and along the shores of small, stream-fed ponds, the muskrat typically constructs its living chamber at the end of a burrow in a nearby bank.

The entrances (usually there are two or three) to this earthen retreat are always below the surface of the water. This greatly limits the number of creatures that can gain access to it. Also, a submerged passageway that is a foot or more underwater is much less likely to freeze, thereby allowing this animal to come and go as it pleases throughout the winter.

While the muskrat is known to cache away some edible items during the autumn for use during the winter months, its stores of food are not sufficient to last for any appreciable length of time. As a result, the muskrat must periodically exit its den and go in search of food.

At this time of the year, foraging consists of methodically digging into the surface of the muck that covers the bottom of the marsh in an attempt to harvest suitable plant and animal matter. The roots of certain types of vegetation, like those of cattails and arrowhead, are highly prized. From mid-autumn until the time when the ice starts to thaw, these roots are concentrated with starches. These complex carbohydrates will eventually be transformed into sugars at the onset of the new growing season, which allows for the redevelopment of these plants when spring arrives. The withered stems of several common marshland plants that formerly covered these waterways are also gathered, as are any seeds that were left by the ducks that seek out such items throughout the summer and autumn. Frogs, salamanders, and even very young turtles that lie dormant in the mud are occasionally encountered by a foraging muskrat and readily consumed, as are freshwater mussels, crayfish, snails, and most other forms of invertebrate life. Unlike the beaver, which is a strict herbivore, the muskrat incorporates a

fair amount of animal matter into its diet, which makes it one of our most omnivorous rodents.

While all of the muskrat's food comes from the bottom during the winter,
none of it is eaten while this creature is submerged. When it finds something to
eat, the muskrat will quickly return with its meal to its den or some other favored
eating site that is out of the water. There always seems to be some hidden cubby
beneath an uprooted tree, in a hollow stump, or in a tiny grotto among a few
rocks clustered together along the shore that can be accessed from under the ice
and utilized as a dining spot.

Under normal conditions, the muskrat dives for several minutes before coming up for air, but this adaptable creature is capable of holding its breath for ten to
twelve minutes if it has to. When traveling under the ice, it frequently relies on
air pockets that develop in various locations to catch its breath. While such oases
of oxygen beneath the surface are often limited in size and number, their locations are believed to be as well known to this creature as is that of the entrance
to its den. Consequently, the muskrat is able to forage for a substantial period of
time without having to surface for air.

The desolate appearance of a frozen lakeshore or ice-bound backwater of a
river often gives the impression that all of its residents have either migrated or
are passing this season in some type of quiescent state. While this is the case for
most creatures, it is not true for the muskrat, which continues its daily routine of
swimming, foraging for food, eating, and resting in the comforts of its shoreline
home throughout this bleak season.

Oxygen Below Ground

In order to maintain life, all living things must be able to absorb oxygen from
their environment. For many creatures, access to fresh air is never a problem,
no matter what the season; however, for some animals, winter can create severe
respiration hardships. Organisms that live below the soil's surface are occasionally confronted with a shortage of oxygen that may become critical as this season
progresses.

While dirt is not generally regarded as being permeable to gases, most soil types have the ability to diffuse small amounts of oxygen some distance below their surface. In summer, there is usually an adequate supply of this essential gas to sustain the myriad forms of life that carry out a subterranean existence. Soil is also able to expel the carbon dioxide and other waste gases that are produced by living organisms, particularly by the actions of bacteria.

As the surface of the soil freezes, its ability to absorb vital atmospheric gases and release those that develop underground diminishes greatly. A covering of snow can also interfere with the exchange of simple molecular vapors. While the depth of this blanket can limit the transfer of gases, its density and condition are far more important factors. Snow that is light and powdery allows for a much better transport of compounds compared to snow that has been saturated on several occasions with rain, then frozen solid.

Mammals that spend the winter in burrows have adapted to this seasonal fluctuation in air quality by greatly reducing their bodies' demand for oxygen in winter. Jumping mice, chipmunks, and woodchucks all enter into a profound period of dormancy, or hibernation, that greatly diminishes their metabolism and likewise lowers their need for oxygen. These critters are often able to survive the winter by utilizing the oxygen that has become trapped in the labyrinth of tunnels and chambers which compose their subterranean domain.

The other small vertebrates that pass the winter in the soil, such as the wood frog, spring peeper, toad, garter snake, and a few species of salamanders, are known to experience an even deeper state of quiescence at this time of year. These creatures require less oxygen to remain alive; they simply rely on the limited amount of air that becomes trapped with them as they wiggle and squirm their way into the dirt of the forest floor during the autumn. Invertebrates, particularly those that are in an egg or pupa stage of their life cycle, need even less oxygen. For these creatures, the shortage of oxygen rarely, if ever, becomes critical.

Moles, which are renowned for their fossorial way of life, are the animals most adversely impacted by the soil's reduction in gas permeability. Because these miniature mammals stay active and maintain a high rate of metabolism throughout the winter, their demand for oxygen remains high. During this season, moles periodically dig their way through the snow pack in order to connect their network of tunnels with the fresh air above. Additionally, excursions to the surface allow a mole to fill its lungs with oxygen-rich air. Moles are believed to be able to function under conditions of extremely low oxygen concentrations by

efficiently processing what little oxygen exists in the air. Similarly, both the beaver and muskrat are known to eat and sleep in enclosed chambers where oxygen levels may drop to only 1 to 2 percent.

Even human animals can experience reduced oxygen in winter. Because modern homes are built to be as airtight as possible, the quality of air indoors during cold Adirondack winters is understandably poorer than in warmer weather when windows are opened. Like the mole, it is important that you get outside regularly during this season and engage in an activity that will "clean out" your lungs. It is also recommended that your heating system should be routinely inspected by a competent individual to ensure that its ventilation is working properly, for unlike the beaver, muskrat, and mole, humans are unable to tolerate too much buildup of carbon dioxide in the environment.

The Subnivean Environment

For our various species of mice, voles, and shrews, typical winter weather in the Adirondacks results in the formation of a favorable microhabitat just below the snow pack. Immediately above the layer of dead leaves and around rotting branches, moss-covered logs, and fern-laden rocks, a low-ceiling world known as the subnivean environment develops when conditions are suitable.

During years when snow accumulates early in the season and an absence of major thaws prevents much melting, the frostline fails to penetrate very deeply into the ground. Snow, especially when it is dry and fluffy, is a most effective thermal barrier. As a result, the temperature of the soil remains around thirty degrees despite the severity of the cold air above.

This near-thawing condition below, coupled with winter's dry air above, stimulates a slow, yet very definite migration of water molecules towards the surface of the snow, despite their still-frozen state. This upward movement of moisture through the ice crystals forms many small openings along the very bottom of the snow pack, resulting in an enhanced living space for those creatures that carry out their existence there. During those years when bitter cold freezes the ground solid early in winter and snowfalls are light and limited, a suitable subnivean setting fails to form. This creates added hardship for the small mammals that rely on it for shelter from the cold and protection from their many natural enemies.

Owls and hawks are the predators that are most adversely impacted by the formation of a subnivean world that keeps mice, voles, and shrews below the surface more than normal. Since these feathered predators lack the ability to sense the presence of small mammals below the snow, they must wait until one eventually comes to the surface. Owls and hawks also lack the ability to quickly dig into the snow to snag a small mammal that has recently retreated into this safer microhabitat. The fox and coyote, however, are still able to detect these rodents' movements using their exceptionally keen sense of hearing – and able to dig down to reach them.

Yet despite the relative warmth and safety afforded by the subnivean environment, mice, voles, and shrews still occasionally venture to the surface for a quick

exposure to the light of day or darkness of night. Researchers that study the ecology of this setting have come up with several theories as to why an animal will make repeated trips to a frigid and dangerous environment.

Some scientists believe that frequent upward movements through the snow create and maintain a network of passageways that allow for an exchange of gases. Even during winter, there is a slow release of carbon dioxide from the soil. To prevent this gas from becoming trapped in the expanse of space beneath the snow pack, these experts believe that ventilating tunnels is essential.

Other biologists suspect that trips to the surface are made in order to get glimpses of daylight. Despite its composition of ice crystals, snow is not entirely transparent, especially after becoming packed down by repeated thaws. (This is why the creatures that reside there have especially sensitive vibrissa, or hairs, that surround their nose. These structures provide them with a sense of touch that is every bit as effective in providing information on where they are and what is around them as is their eyesight.)

While seeing the sun is certainly an uplifting experience for humans, it is an important biological need for animals that depend on internal light clocks for regulating events in their lives. It is photoperiodism, rather than a response to the prevailing weather conditions, that governs the cycles in many creatures, and it just may be that animals living in the subnivean world need to frequently set their biological clocks by noting where the sun is, or when the eastern sky begins to brighten in the morning.

Other naturalists claim that it is simply "cabin fever." Even though they are relatively safe and warm, these animals, like humans, periodically experience a need to get out of their nests and confined living spaces and bask in the fresh air and openness of the world above, with the hope that spring is not too far away.

Bad Tasting Shrews and Moles

The sight of any small animal suddenly appearing on the surface of the snow instinctively triggers an attack response in virtually all of the predators that inhabit the Adirondacks during the winter. Because of the scarcity of prey during this season and the need to generate a tremendous amount of body heat, the act of immediately killing whatever it sees has become the carnivores' primary means of survival. Yet not all of the victims of these wildlife encounters are eaten, as moles and shrews are occasionally rejected because of their exceptionally bad taste.

Both of these pint-sized, slate-gray animals belong to a group of mammals known as insectivores. As the name implies, shrews and moles feed primarily on invertebrate matter, particularly that which abounds beneath the leaf litter covering the forest floor and below the soil's surface. Because these creatures rely entirely on a sense of smell to locate food amidst the soil and dead organic debris on the ground, the ability to detect and decipher odors is especially well developed in these miniature mammals.

Moles and shrews also use their keen olfactory senses to pick up fragrance and smells emitted by other moles and shrews. Like several other creatures, these animals depend entirely on scent-producing glands to communicate territorial intentions and breeding status to neighboring animals. These glands, located just below their skin, and the chemicals they emit are believed to give a repulsive taste to their carcasses. As a result, neither is specifically hunted by the predators of our region that ordinarily target such mouse-sized animals.

In winter, however, predators do not have the luxury to be selective in what they kill, and they become increasingly indiscriminate in their attacks on small animals as the season progresses. Once one of these animals is sighted on the surface, a bobcat, fisher, marten, or owl will kill first and then decide if it wants to eat it. A fox or coyote, both of which depend more on the sounds produced by small mammals as they move through the frozen matter under the snow than on sight to locate their prey, will also act immediately upon detecting a potential meal. Both of these canines skillfully pounce on the spot from which the faint noise is coming and immediately dig down to their quarry. Should a mole or shrew be the victim of a successful attack, the catch may be dropped when a first taste is obtained after being crushed between their powerful jaws.

During times when hunting becomes difficult during deep snow conditions or when prey is scarce, nearly all animals are believed to reluctantly eat both moles and shrews. Young, inexperienced predators that are confronted with the harsh realities of a bleak landscape for the first time also will routinely eat them, as hunger is a powerful stimulus. But in cases where mice, voles, squirrels, varying hares, birds, and other small game are plentiful, both of these insectivores are usually left at the spot where they were killed.

A dead shrew or mole may be seen lying on the surface by those traveling through a snow-bound forest. This is usually not an individual that has succumbed to starvation or hypothermia, as such victims of our harsh northern climate ordinarily perish in some sheltered retreat or nest. Rather, the lifeless carcass is a sure sign that there is a skilled predator in the area, one that has been successful enough at taking other types of game that it hasn't had to resort to consuming the nearly unpalatable carcass of a mole or shrew.

The Gray Jay

Included in the very short list of birds that can exist year-round in the coldest and most inhospitable environments of the Adirondacks is a resourceful creature known as the gray jay. Despite the harshness of the climate and the limited sources of food on the upper slopes of our mountains and in the frigid hollows that contain bogs, the gray jay is able to eke out an existence in these boreal settings.

While it is nearly identical in size to the blue jay, the gray jay lacks the crested head that is so characteristic of its close relative. Also, as its name implies, this species of jay is mostly grayish, rather than bluish-purple, in color. Because of its coloring and a prominent dark patch on the back of its head, the gray jay may be mistaken at first glance for a greatly enlarged chickadee. However, its white throat and forehead can easily be used to distinguish it from those friendly birds that often flock around feeders.

Like other jays, the gray jay has a thick and pointed bill that is adapted for pecking at and pulling apart pieces of animal matter. During the summer, this opportunistic feeder is known to kill young birds that have been left unattended in their nest for a few moments while both parents are out gathering food. It also feasts on the various fruits, seeds, and insects that are available this time of year in the dense spruce and fir forests in which it resides.

As these sources of food dwindle with the approach of winter, the gray jay becomes one of this region's most effective scavengers. Animal carcasses are sought out, then picked clean of any shreds of fat and flesh.

In its attempt to locate such items, the gray jay is believed to watch and follow the movements of the common predators that likewise reside in boreal forests. Both the fisher and marten, two secretive members of the weasel family, are extremely adept at finding and killing red squirrels, grouse, mice, voles, and varying hares, and the fisher also satisfies its appetite by preying on porcupines. In low elevation conifer forests, such as the dense stands of black spruce and fir that surround bogs and the shores of slow-moving streams, the gray jay often spends time watching the movements of a coyote, fox, or bobcat, as once a kill is made by one of these carnivores, there are inevitably some leftovers lying around.

When it witnesses a kill, this jay will closely approach the scene, especially if the hunter has dismembered its quarry and is contentedly gnawing a chunk of the carcass. On occasions, it will dart in to steal any morsel that it can grab hold of, and then quickly take off before being attacked itself. More frequently, the jay simply waits until after its provider has had its fill and leaves the scene, at which time it will devour any scraps that may remain, including drops of blood that dot the snow. It will also pick at the carcass of a mole or shrew that was rejected by its killer because of its unappealing taste.

This jay's boldness around scraps of food during the winter became legendary in the logging camps that flourished in the Adirondacks well over a century ago. It was known to frequent these outposts of civilization deep in the wilderness and help itself to any food that became available. Stories abound about the gray jay's daring raids on the plates of woodsmen who were snacking outdoors.

Should you travel through an upper elevation setting or meander into a low-

land spruce-fir forest, you may happen to notice one of these large, chickadee-like birds. Don't expect to see one, however, around a feeder located within one of the towns or villages of the Adirondacks, as the gray jay seldom visits such settings. Even during the dead of winter, this bird seems capable of finding enough scraps to eat, including the remains of those creatures that have fallen victim to the murderous winter weather.

The Snowy Owl

Despite the severity of the weather during this season, the North Country serves as a winter retreat for several species of birds that migrate from the Arctic. Occasionally included among these visitors from the far North is the snowy owl, one of the tundra's largest and most impressive birds of prey.

Like many Arctic inhabitants, the snowy owl is predominantly white, although most individuals also possess noticeable dark spots. The degree of contrasting color can be helpful in identifying the age and sex of an individual. Juveniles have the greatest concentration of spots, as these sizeable dark patches may cover nearly one-half of their body and form conspicuous patterns of brownish streaks. Adult females have a lesser degree of dark patches near the ends of their feathers, and adult males have fewer still. As the males age, their spotted pattern fades and may eventually disappear altogether. As a result, a snowy owl that is almost completely white can be identified as an older male.

Unlike most owls, this bird often hunts during the day rather than at night. Because of the absence of darkness in the high latitudes for most of the spring and summer, the snowy owl has evolved mainly into a diurnal predator. With the return of the long Arctic nights, many snowy owls begin to journey south where the length of daylight is more favorable. Also, because most small Arctic mammals and birds either hibernate or migrate during this season, this predator is left with little to hunt other than lemmings. During years when the population of these vole-like rodents is high, most snowy owls remain in their usual habitat for as long as they are successful in finding food. Unrelenting cold and darkness can be tolerated by this bird of prey provided it has plenty of meat to eat. An exceptionally dense covering of feathers insulates it against the frigid air, and while it prefers to hunt in daylight, it does have the ability to take prey at night, especially when conditions are such that its chances for success are high.

When the number of lemmings is low, nearly all snowy owls retreat southward in search of areas where small game is more abundant. It is during these years of low lemming populations when the appearance of this impressive creature becomes widespread throughout northern and central New York. Since the arctic tundra is flat and treeless, the snowy owl is drawn to settings that offer the same environmental features. Large open areas, such as the agricultural fields and pastures that occur throughout the Champlain, St. Lawrence, Hudson, and Mohawk valleys, are most attractive to this bird. The mountainous terrain and dense forests of the Central Adirondacks are avoided, yet the snowy owl has periodically been reported around golf courses, airports, and other similar flat, open places within the Park.

Once it finds a place where it can repeatedly kill small creatures, the snowy owl will remain there for the entire winter. Should food eventually become scarce, its nomadic inclination causes it to move again in search of a more favorable hunting site.

While food in our region may remain plentiful throughout the late winter and on into the spring, an ever increasing urge to breed causes the snowy owl to abandon its wintering grounds. Mature adults that want to lay claim to prime nesting sites are the first to venture back north. Younger birds that have not yet reached sexual maturity may linger well into April before starting their journey to the Arctic.

It is not uncommon for people who live in relatively flat, open places to think that the Arctic is outside their window as the gales of January continuously sweep snow over the treeless landscape. Along with the inhospitable weather, the appearance of one of the tundra's most attractive predators can confirm the notion that, during the dead of winter, our landscape can be nearly identical to the snow-covered terrain well to the north.

Tracks in the Snow

To the hardy outdoor enthusiast, snow is essential for making the landscape into a winter playground. To the curious-minded naturalist, snow is also a critical component of this season, for it provides a way to gather information on the presence, abundance, habitats, and haunts of those forms of wildlife that trek across its surface.

Developing the ability to identify animal tracks is not difficult to do, as the most common members of our winter wildlife community create imprints that possess enough unique characteristics to be easy to recognize (and numerous guides and charts exist for those who want some help).

The red fox, for example, walks by placing its legs directly under its body. This forms a pattern of paw prints that are virtually in a straight line. Only the domestic cat produces a similar pattern, yet a cat's paws are smaller and rounder than those of the fox, which are roughly the size of a half dollar and are more elongated in shape. Additionally, under good conditions, the toenails of a fox can be noted at the front of its tracks, while a cat keeps its claws pulled into its paws when it walks, thereby forming a set of tracks in which nail prints are absent.

The coyote places its feet a short distance to the right and left of each side of its body as it walks. This leaves a collection of imprints that are slightly off center of the line in which the animal was traveling. Because of the width of the chest of a domestic dog, its feet are separated by an even greater distance when they come into contact with the ground. This results in a very noticeable set of right and left paw prints. Also, like the fox, a coyote's foot is slightly longer than it is wide, while the paw of a domestic dog measures the same in both directions when placed in the snow.

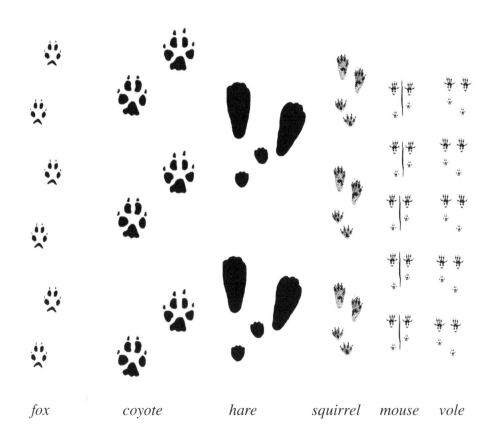

fox   coyote   hare   squirrel   mouse   vole

In dense entanglements of conifers and along the edges of alder-choked streams and brush-covered swamps, the tracks of the varying hare are common. Unlike the fox, coyote, deer, and other game animals, the hare, known to many as the snowshoe rabbit, does not place its hind feet in the space vacated by its front paws. Rather, it swings its enlarged hind feet ahead of its forepaws, creating a tract pattern that clearly shows all four of its feet.

In settings covered with maturing evergreens, the tracks of the red squirrel may be regularly seen crisscrossing the snow's surface. Like the varying hare, this rodent leaves behind a set of tracks that shows all four of its feet. Since it holds its front legs closer together, it creates a set of tracks in which two side-by-side paw prints are followed by another two that are spaced a slightly greater distance apart.

Found just as much around homes as in remote wilderness areas, the tiny imprints left by mice are also easy to identify. When mice emerge on the surface to travel to a particular spot, they ordinarily jump or leap, rather than walk. Since a quick-paced movement minimizes the time that they are exposed to the view of their many natural enemies, this bounding gate is important for survival. Additionally, jumping is sometimes the only way in which these small rodents are able to effectively propel themselves forward through the snow, especially when the surface contains several inches of light fluff.

When springing forward, mice push with both of their hind legs simultaneously. This produces a track pattern that is composed of sets of miniature footprints that are side by side. Also, as they leap upward, their tail inevitably drags behind them. This etches a small, yet noticeable, rut between the tracks left by their feet.

19

Voles, which are nearly identical in size to mice and are just about as abundant, make a similar track pattern in the snow. Like their relatives, voles are forced to employ a bounding motion in order to move quickly over a powdery surface. However, because a vole's tail is considerably shorter, the line it creates in the snow is correspondingly smaller, and in some cases may be totally absent.

Aside from telling which animals have been in the area, tracks have various subtleties that enable an expert naturalist to gain added information. For example, by assessing their freshness, it is sometimes possible to tell when they were made. How large they are and how far apart they are spaced can provide clues to the size of the animal and whether it was walking, trotting, or running. The setting from which the tracks came and the area they are passing through yield information on the creature's habitat preference. Aside from giving the surface a more detailed appearance, tracks provide an excellent record of what has recently occurred in the immediate area for those who are able to read and interpret these wildlife signs.

Supercooled Bugs

The prolonged periods of intense cold that can settle over the Adirondacks are understandably very hard on those forms of life that remain active during this season. However, the severity and duration of the cold also has a major impact on the survival of those invertebrates that pass the winter in a state of dormancy.

In order to survive, some lower forms of life must escape the thermal harshness of this season by burrowing beneath the frost line or embedding themselves in the muck that covers the bottom of aquatic settings. Others simply seek shelter in the various cracks and crevices on the bark of trees and shrubs, and in clumps of dried grass, weeds and ferns. These creatures have evolved the means of contending with bitter cold by developing a physiology that is tolerant of temperatures that drop well below freezing.

Prior to entering their dormant period, bugs that overwinter above ground gradually reduce the concentration of water in their bodies. Since this causes water molecules to be spaced further apart, it decreases the likelihood that they will combine to create a crystalline form. This is like the suppression of the freezing point of water in the radiator of a car as antifreeze is added. Excess food that is consumed during the summer and autumn is transformed into a type of fat known as glycerol. This lipid, in suitable concentrations, is instrumental in preventing water molecules from combining together in cells.

Bugs also lower the risk of freezing by reducing their intake of foreign matter. In order for water to solidify, it must first have something onto which its molecules can attach to form a crystal. Such substances are known as crystallization nuclei, and dust, along with a collection of other compounds that are normally ingested both on and within their food, serves as such nuclei. Therefore, as

21

the number of these particles decrease inside a bug, it becomes less likely that ice will develop within it and cause death. Consequently, when exposed to severe cold, the moisture in a bug's tissue develops into a supercooled state, but it does not freeze.

However, as any chemist will attest, if a solution is cooled to a low enough temperature and held there for a sufficient period of time, crystallization will inevitably occur. Even in the absence of any nuclei, water molecules will combine and form ice when their alignment becomes favorable. As winter drags on, the odds are that an increasingly greater number of invertebrates that pass this season in a supercooled state will develop ice within their bodies and freeze. During years when winter ends early (at least from an Adirondack perspective), mortality among these bugs is relatively low. Should this season linger well beyond what is normal, death will be far more prevalent.

Because of the severity and duration of winter in the Adirondacks, some invertebrates have developed a tolerance for internal ice crystals. Consequently, these bugs are able to carry out the various processes needed to sustain life during their dormant stage despite the presence of frozen water in their system.

Mortality can be very high among nearly all forms of wildlife when frigid air becomes entrenched over the region for a seemingly endless period of time. Yet enough bugs survive the season to reestablish viable populations when conditions become favorable in the spring.

A final note: Because black flies overwinter under the ice, they are not as adversely impacted by the intensity and duration of a bitterly cold air mass as are bugs that pass this season above ground. While excessive ice formation on stream bottoms may cause some mortality, it does not destroy as many of these dormant insects as most people would like. As a result, regardless of how severe this season may be, there will still be an ample number of black flies when mid-May finally arrives.

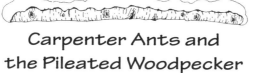

Carpenter Ants and the Pileated Woodpecker

The intense cold and excessive dryness of the air that prevails across the Adirondacks in winter causes all insects to seek out some type of shelter. For carpenter ants, this protection is provided by the numerous chambers that lie deep within the wood of trees.

Like termites, carpenter ants are well known for their ability to create a labyrinth of tunnels and cavities as they chew their way through wood. However, unlike termites, which target any type of wood, these sizeable black- and tan-colored ants prefer to bore only into material that is fairly moist and soft. Dead trees and stumps that have just begun to decompose are their favored haunts, as are sections of trunks, branches, and exposed roots of apparently healthy trees, which are experiencing problems with internal decay. Unfortunately, carpenter ants are also known to establish colonies in the beams and timbers of a house if they become wet in spring and remain relatively moist throughout the summer, as well as in those that have undergone some degree of dry rot. Dry wood in well-ventilated and properly-maintained homes is avoided by new queens when they search for places to establish colonies during the late spring.

Also unlike termites, carpenter ants do not consume any of this woody tissue.

Rather, these insects feed on small bits and pieces of animal matter that are present in these surroundings. During the late summer and early autumn, carpenter ants will eat as much as possible in an attempt to build a deposit of fat, which is necessary to help prevent them from freezing and to fuel their life processes throughout the winter.

As the time for their winter dormancy arrives, the adults gather into clusters in various locations in the colony. By congregating into large masses, these invertebrates are able to help conserve body warmth and reduce the rate at which they lose moisture to their surroundings. However, while developing fat and gathering into a sizeable mass helps ensure their survival in our northern climate, it also makes them a perfect food source for the pileated woodpecker, a crow-sized bird that is mostly black with distinct white and red markings.

By rapping its bill against various parts of a tree, a pileated woodpecker is able to determine if there is a colony somewhere within that structure and zero in on its location. Once it has pinpointed a potential food source, this bird then

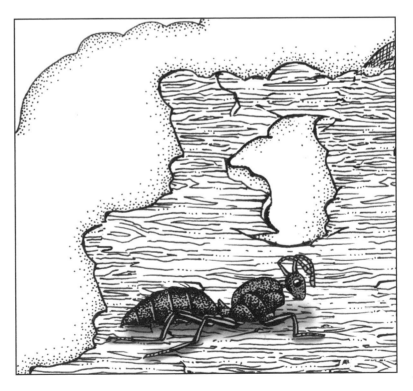

begins to chip and chisel away at the bark and outer wood. As clusters of these nutritious ants are uncovered, they are immediately pulled into the woodpecker's mouth by its specially-adapted tongue.

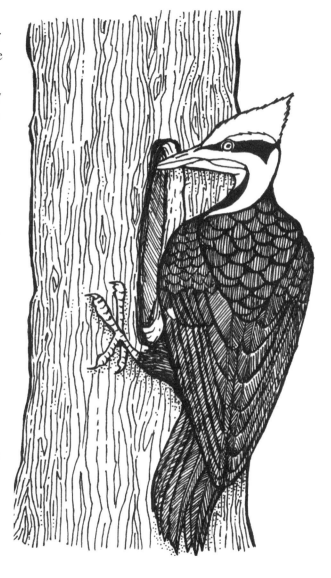

While recently-established colonies are small and may provide this bird with enough food for only a single meal, those that have been in place for longer periods of time can be quite substantial. Such large clusters allow for repeated visits and result in the excavation of sizeable holes in a tree. Since the ants are dormant at this time of year, there is little if any reaction to an attack by a pileated woodpecker. The high concentration of formic acid in these ants makes them quite unpalatable to other foraging birds such as chickadees and nuthatches. It is the pileated woodpecker that has adapted the unique taste for these insects.

When one is hiking, snowshoeing, or cross-country skiing in the Adirondacks, it is not uncommon to see chunks of bark and small pieces of wood scattered on the snow around the base of a tree. Should this debris be from a sizeable cavity that extends several inches into a tree, it is clear evidence that a pileated wood-pecker is residing in the vicinity, doing its job of controlling the numbers of wood-dwelling ants that are plentiful in our forests even during the dead of winter.

The Crossbills

According to the theory of natural selection developed by Charles Darwin, the bills of all birds have evolved over eons to best suit the needs of their particular species. For example, the pileated woodpecker has developed a bill that can withstand the repeated blows which it routinely delivers to the trunks of trees in order to plunder colonies of carpenter ants. The crossbills, a small group of birds that belong to the finch family, support another type of highly specialized beak that allows them to take advantage of a different source of food that is present in the Adirondacks during the winter.

The crossbill is so named because of the way in which its upper mandible curves and hooks over its lower counterpart. This crossed design, which gives the mouth of these birds a somewhat deformed appearance, is ideal for ripping open the cones that are produced by our numerous softwood trees. Upon encountering one of these woody structures on a pine, fir, or spruce tree, a crossbill inserts the pointed tips of its unopened bill into the tiny slot created by the end of one of the cone's scales. When the bird's mouth opens, the crossed mandibles twist the covering and pry it upward, exposing the small, winged seed encased within. The crossbill then extracts this flat, papery structure from the cone with its tongue and promptly swallows it. By rapidly repeating this procedure on each of the other scales composing the cone, and then on other nearby cones, a crossbill is able to consume a sizeable amount of seeds in a relatively short span of time.

Unlike most members of the finch family, a crossbill does not extract the tiny kernel of embryonic life and stored food from its papery shuck before swallowing it. Rather, it gulps down as many complete seeds as possible, filling a specially adapted crop located in its throat. Once this unique structure is packed with seeds, the bird retreats to a place that affords greater protection from the wind, as it is often quite breezy at the tops of trees where cones are most abundant. The ingested seeds are then gradually regurgitated and properly shucked in the bird's mouth. This manner of quickly gathering food and then chewing it later in a protected place also reduces the bird's chances of being seen and attacked by a predator. A crossbill's crop holds an exceptionally large quantity of food for a bird of its size. By packing the sac with seeds just before dusk, the crossbill is better able to survive the very lengthy nights of a northern winter.

Since evergreen trees abound in colder climates, crossbills are generally restricted to more northern latitudes. And the fact that most conifers support cones on their twigs throughout the winter is another reason that these birds don't need to migrate as colder weather intensifies during the autumn.

Like the crops of wild berries that form in open, brush-covered settings, the quality of a cone crop will vary greatly from one year to the next depending on weather conditions. If an area experienced numerous late frosts, an extended drought, or prolonged bouts of cold and cloudy weather during the initial period of seed development, then chances are that the crop will either be severely lim-

27

ited or non-existent. Because of this variability, crossbills do not become permanent residents of any one particular area, as do chickadees or nuthatches. Rather, these grosbeak-sized birds have developed a more nomadic pattern of travel that causes them to take up residence in any conifer setting that currently possesses a rich supply of seeds.

Like the warblers during the summer, the crossbills are not easy birds to spot. Since their bill is poorly adapted for opening the shucks that encase a sunflower seed, these birds cannot be enticed to a feeder as other seed eaters can at this time of the year. Also, since many cones are located in the upper half of larger trees, crossbills are unlikely to be encountered close to the ground where a person could get a good look at them. Instead, they remain hidden among the dense needles of the canopy.

Although crossbills are not among the most familiar of winter birds, they are common in the dense stands of evergreens which cover so much of northern New York, especially during those years when a warm, moist spring and a good, long summer created conditions that lead to a bumper crop of conifer seeds.

The Nuthatches

It is almost guaranteed that if you maintain a bird feeder with plenty of sunflower seeds during the winter in the northeast, a nuthatch or two will be included in the regular parade of daily visitors to your home. With its rather stout build, short, stubby tail, and long, narrow, pointed bill, the nuthatch is among the easiest of birds to recognize. Also, the unique manner in which it creeps in an inverted position down the trunk of a tree and awkwardly clings to the underside of a limb or twig make it easy to spot as well as a delight to watch.

Like the chickadee, the nuthatch obtains its nourishment during the winter by consuming an assortment of seeds and foraging on various forms of invertebrate matter that it can extract from cracks and crevices under the bark of trees. Unlike the chickadee, which scours the lower sections of such nooks and crannies while it works its way up the tree, the nuthatch probes the upper parts of such surface irregularities while creeping down the trunk. Its long and slender bill is ideally adapted for reaching into the places where many of our bugs pass this season.

The types of seeds which a nuthatch collects – other than those that it takes from a feeder – depends upon the species. The white-breasted nuthatch is an expert at finding tree seeds that have not yet become covered with snow, particularly in warm valley areas where hardwoods dominate the landscape. Occasionally, after retrieving a fairly hard seed, this bird is known to bring it to a crotch in a tree, wedge it there, and begin to rap on it with its bill in an attempt to crack open or hatch the nut (hence its name).

The red-breasted nuthatch exhibits a definite preference for evergreen forests, as it has a knack for prying the tiny, winged seeds from cones, especially those of the pines and spruces. Since conifers are more abundant in colder areas, the red-breasted nuthatch is more northern in its distribution and more common throughout the Central Adirondacks than its slightly larger cousin. During years when the cone crop fails, the red-breasted nuthatch migrates southward until it locates an area in which there is a suitable supply of seeds.

While the nuthatch appears to be as friendly as the chickadee, its pleasant temperament extends only to humans and its black-capped associates. Unlike most of our winter avian residents, the nuthatch does not tolerate other nuthatches in the immediate vicinity, except for former or future breeding partners. This is why the nuthatch is never seen in a flock of its own kind. When it feels the need to gain the protection that comes in traveling with and feeding in a group, it will readily join up with a flock of chickadees rather than seek the company of other nuthatches. It is only during the winter that a white-breasted nuthatch may be regularly seen in the presence of another white-breasted nuthatch. This would be a male and female that have already established a mating bond for the coming spring breeding season, and there will be no more than these two individuals in that same general area.

Unlike other birds, nuthatches spend the night roosting inside the cavity of a tree. Ordinarily, such holes are the result of a woodpecker's handiwork or the action of bacteria rotting away the inside of a diseased tree trunk. As dusk approaches each evening, the nuthatch faithfully returns to its own wooden enclosure, which helps protect it against the cold of our long winter nights. As daylight reappears the following morning, the nuthatch will exit its home to begin the daily foraging routine that is sure to include a stop at someone's feeder, if it is fortunate enough to have one within the confines of its winter range.

Singing Chickadees

One of the very first signs of spring for ornithologists is the return of the pleasant-sounding mating call of the black-capped chickadee. On those picturesque mornings during mid-winter when the air is perfectly still and the haze that has formed overnight becomes illuminated by the sun, the chickadee starts to sing its distinctive breeding song.

Unlike many Adirondack birds, the chickadee has a rather extensive vocal repertoire. Throughout the autumn and winter, its familiar "chick-a-dee-dee-dee" call can be heard as a flock slowly works it way through a stand of evergreen trees. Occasionally, this black, gray, and off-white bird will also utter a series of "dee-dee-dee-dee" notes, particularly if one member of the flock is upset about some facet of its surroundings. Various other vocalizations made by the chickadee may be heard throughout the year, and each of its songs has its own special meaning to the members of its flock. However, none of its calls are as clear sounding or carry as well as its mating song.

As spring draws closer, the male begins to practice the simple two-note, whistling song commonly described as "feeee-bee." The first note of this call is noticeably higher in pitch and slightly longer in duration than the second. The second note is composed of a sound that drops off in intensity as the song ends. Occasionally, it is modified into a three-note segment, creating a song that resembles the phrase "feeee-be-be."

Like that of many perching birds, the mating call is used by the male to proclaim his dominance in a specific area and draw the attention of a potential breeding partner. Since chickadees will continue to stay together in a flock for several more months, the "feeee-bee" call of one individual typically stimulates another male in the flock to emit an identical song, thereby proclaiming his presence and superior fitness for eventual breeding. Occasionally, a third male may add its voice to this musical display, resulting in a random chorus of songs.

During February, this mating call is only trilled during the early morning and always coincides with periods of bright, sunny weather. However, by March and throughout April, this song is heard far more frequently, as it may be sung during the middle of the day and under a variety of weather conditions.

As the time for nesting nears, the older birds in the winter flock begin to more physically exercise their dominance over those individuals that are subordinate to them in the group. Eventually, the dominant male and female establish a pair bond with one another and lay claim to the best section of the winter range, excluding all others. The next male and female in the flock's hierarchy also normally pair up and claim much of the remaining land. Occasionally, there

may be enough space left over for a third pair of chickadees, but more often than not, these individuals are forced to look elsewhere for a place to establish as a breeding territory. Since mortality can claim more than half of the members of a winter flock, it is not uncommon for only two or three pairs of birds to survive to the onset of the spring breeding season.

From this time until the end of April, chickadees will remain together and continue to forage in the mixed and softwood forests. While the weather remains cold and blustery winds create bitter conditions, these social birds engage almost exclusively in activities related to their survival. On those occasions when a small amount of time and energy can be spared from battling the weather, males begin to advertise their presence with a song that will catch the attention of a female chickadee, as well as delighting of all those who enjoy listening to nature's music.

The Howling Coyote

In early to mid-February, the yelping howl of the coyote may be heard more frequently than during previous months, especially during the early evening and late at night. While some people may associate this increased vocal activity with the nearing of a full moon, it is actually the approach of this carnivore's mating season that is responsible for its renewed interest in singing, not a reaction to any increase in lunar illumination.

Once this sizeable wild dog begins to experience the urge to breed, its focus of attention is the individual of the opposite sex with which it shares a specific parcel of land. As February progresses, these two adults spend increasingly greater amounts of time together. Because of the dense nature of our forests, it is quite common for the two to become separated when they travel in search of food. Consequently, they make frequent attempts to locate one another by loudly announcing their whereabouts and then homing in on the response.

Throughout the autumn and for most of the winter, food acquisition is the prime concern of the pair, and defending their territory is less important. However, the intrusion of another adult, particularly a male, not only creates added competition for game within the general area, but also poses a challenge to the resident coyote for the right to breed with the other adult occupant of that area. As a result, the boundaries of a territory are patrolled more regularly as mating season approaches and are repeatedly marked in an attempt to dissuade any wandering individuals from entering.

A coyote will loudly proclaim its willingness to track down and physically confront any trespasser by announcing ownership of his territory to all coyotes that are within shouting, or howling, distance. Consequently, the barking cries that echo across the hillsides and valleys during mid-winter are also attempts by a resident to assert its dominance over that area.

Maturing pups that have been allowed to remain in a parent's territory up to now (because of their assistance in hunting and bringing down deer) may or may not be forced to leave. As is the case with the wolf, these individuals are sometimes permitted to share the same area and become members of the pack, as long as they remain subordinate to the adults that have established themselves on that site and do not show any interest in breeding. Should one of these maturing individuals express a desire to mate or attempt to feed alongside an adult, it will be attacked and forced to submit to the rules of the pack, or it will be driven away.

As the dominant female in the area comes into heat, which is believed to be during the middle part of February in the Adirondacks, the frequency of the coyote's yelping howls reaches a climax and then gradually tapers off into early to mid-March. The gestation period for these close cousins of the wolf is two full

months. Thus, while the weather is typically quite harsh during the brief breeding season, it inevitably is far more pleasant when the pups are born. It is around this time when food is becoming more plentiful and easier for an experienced predator to acquire. This, then, is the time when a lactating female can most effectively satisfy her increased hunger.

It is not until several weeks after birth that the pups develop to the stage at which they begin to emerge from the entrance of their den and start to explore their surroundings. By this time it is usually early May, and this new generation of pups will soon begin to add their voices to the serenade of the adults that can be heard in virtually every part of the Adirondacks, regardless of whether there is a full moon or not.

Winter Scent Posts

The phrase "Don't eat yellow snow!" is sound advice for us all, as such discolored patches on the ground obviously contain substances that should not be ingested. However, for most forms of wildlife, these excrement sites are highly attractive and must be carefully investigated, especially at this time of the year.

By mid-February, coyotes, fox, bobcats, and skunks are rapidly entering their breeding season in the Adirondacks. As a result, their territorial behavior reaches a peak, and the boundaries of the land claimed by individuals or pairs become more widely advertised.

Scent posts are the primary means nearly all mammals use to stake their claim to a particular parcel of property, and urine is the most commonly used substance for establishing these olfactory markers. In order to maximize the chances that a neighbor or wandering juvenile will detect these "no trespassing" signs, their placement is highly concentrated around the periphery of a territory. During this time of the year, it is not uncommon to see such yellow-stained patches every hundred yards or so, connected by the tracks of the owner. During a prolonged period when additional snow does not fall, these boundary markers remain visible and may be easily noted by a perceptive individual. Although a dusting of snow will obliterate all visual evidence of such markers, their scent is potent enough to remain effective beneath a thin layer of white powder.

The amount of time that passes before the resident must retrace its property line in order to refresh the scent posts varies depending on the weather. A mid-winter rainstorm or a nor'easter that dumps a substantial accumulation of snow can quickly obliterate the chemical signature an owner places on its territory, while a fast-moving clipper system that may bring only an inch or two of powder usually does little to diminish its effectiveness.

Since no mammal can produce an endless supply of this amber fluid, only very small amounts are ever discharged at any one time and at any given location. Animals are also very careful to place their scent where it will be most easily detected. Objects that are at nose height, such as short stumps, the side of a snow bank, or low tree limbs are usually targeted for a shot of urine. Such slightly elevated sites also improve the chances that a passing animal will see one of these patches of discolored snow.

As an animal travels toward the center of its territory, the frequency of these scent posts is believed to drop off drastically. As a result, a juvenile that is currently searching for a home of its own can determine both where a boundary exists and how far it may be straying into another's piece of real estate. Similarly, a person encountering a set of tracks may assess the general location by noting the presence or absence of scent posts when following tracks for less than a quarter mile.

Upon spotting a patch of yellow snow, wildlife researchers and naturalists may look to see if there are any nose prints in or around that patch. Such a subtle disturbance of the snow often indicates that a neighboring animal has also passed by and investigated the spot. Occasionally, the owner of the adjacent parcel of land will add its own scent to that site in order to reaffirm its control of the property on the opposite side of the line.

Scat is also used to establish and maintain boundaries. Like urine, solid excrement is always deposited in a spot where it is most likely to be detected by other individuals. Occasionally, both the fox and coyote will also scratch at the ground around a site that has recently been marked. Researchers are of the opinion that this is done to deposit the additional scent that develops in the areas of its paws between its toes.

As spring draws near and the snow begins to melt, the yellow patches that are so significant to these mammals start to fade from view, but scent posts continue to be maintained well into the spring. Although they are now invisible, these chemical markers remain evident to any and all creatures with a keen and discerning sense of smell.

The Bobcat's Breeding Season

The sound of a loud, piercing scream is enough to send your heart rate and blood pressure through the roof, especially if you are alone and are miles out in the woods. However, such an unnerving, high-pitched shriek at this time of the year is likely not coming from a person; it is the call of a bobcat that wants to draw the attention of a mate.

Like several other forms of wildlife, the bobcat is entering its breeding season during the very end of February, and one means that it uses to advertise its presence is a vocalization that can carry for a substantial distance.

In semi-open settings in a milder, temperate climate, or on a brush-covered hillside in a desert, which are the preferred habitats of the bobcat, its screaming cry is capable of carrying over a mile, particularly on a clear and calm night. But amidst the snow-covered boughs of an evergreen thicket, which are excellent at absorbing sound, this blood curdling wail is seldom able to travel several hundred yards before its energy is totally lost. Consequently, the bobcat must also rely heavily on its scent posts to advertise its presence. It is believed by some naturalists that its chemical emissions are more important in initially drawing two potential mates to the same general area within the Central Adirondacks than in any of the other geographic regions it populates.

The very limited populations of small game available to the bobcat during the winter in northern New York and its lack of mobility in deep snow cause it to look for deer as its primary source of meat. Since the whitetail migrates to low-lying conifer forests as winter sets in to better cope with the rigors of this season, the bobcat also concentrates much of its time in these ecological settings.

Residing in evergreen lowlands also increases the bobcat's chances of encountering one of the varying hares which inhabit this setting, although the hare has a definite advantage over the bobcat when running on snow. However, when the rare opportunity does present itself, the bobcat is quick to pounce on the meaty, small-game creature.

While the bobcat would have an almost impossible time bringing down a healthy whitetail, this carnivore possesses the skills and strength to take a winter-weakened individual. Also, while the bobcat prefers to kill its own food, it is not averse to scavenging the carcass of a deer that succumbed to starvation.

The presence of sick and malnourished deer in the Adirondacks is believed to be the main reason the bobcat is able to exist in this northern region. If this food source were unavailable, the chances are that these skillful hunters would not be able to find enough prey during the bleak days of winter to remain alive and maintain a viable population.

For young, inexperienced bobcats, winter poses the ultimate challenge of

survival, and it is one which many of them fail. Those that are successful during their first year of life continue to develop and hone their hunting skills and attack tactics. If a bobcat is successful in killing or scavenging four to six deer throughout the winter, its mating urge will awaken as it nears the age of two, and it will begin its search for a breeding partner.

Despite the relatively low numbers of bobcats in the Adirondacks, the chances of two of these solitary creatures finding one another is considered to be good. Since they are concentrated in the same general area in and around deer yards during the onset of the breeding season, their paths will eventually cross. Also, the scent posts which they produce and the chemical trail which they leave behind is believed to greatly increase the likelihood that a male and female will encounter one another. Finally, the screams a bobcat gives when it senses the presence of another nearby will ultimately bring the two face-to-face, thereby starting the process that leads to a future generation of these handsome and wily predators.

March

The Color Of Spring

The approach of spring brings some subtle yet definite changes to the color of the hillsides, mountain ridges, and shorelines that are covered by deciduous forests. From the time these trees shed their leaves in October until a week or two prior to St. Patrick's Day, North Country landscapes that are cloaked with hardwood trees display a grayish hue that creates a bleakly stark impression. However, as average daytime temperatures begin to rise above freezing and the sun's rays become increasingly more intense, many forests, particularly those on south-facing slopes, develop a light, reddish cast or a faint, olive-green tint. This is the first visible indication that the forest is gradually awakening from its winter dormancy.

It is during March that sunlight finally gains enough intensity to begin thawing the cells in tree trunks, even though the temperature of the air may remain below freezing. The heat absorbed by a trunk inevitably radiates outward and starts to melt the snow around its base. By late March, noticeable rings of bare ground have formed around nearly all tree trunks, regardless of the amount of snow that still covers the forest floor.

Eventually, as the soil around the base of a tree also begins to thaw, it becomes free to absorb the water produced from the melting snow. The increase in moisture in the soil stimulates the roots, and in a short period of time, these

underground structures are taking in water and forming sap.

Sap only flows into the trunk after being adequately warmed. It then continues its upward movement into the smaller structures as warm air reacts with the
branches and twigs. When the sap finally reaches the buds, it stimulates internal
processes that result in both a slight swelling and a subtle color change to the
twig tips.

For the quaking aspen, the gradual return of sap into its trunk and branches
causes the photosynthetic cells that are contained in its bark to be revitalized.
Unlike most hardwoods, the quaking aspen possesses a layer of tissue that
contains chlorophyll, enabling this sun-loving tree to carry out the manufacture
of food well before its leaves erupt later in the season. And while these cells lie
hidden beneath a corky exterior that is covered by a film of white powder, their
presence begins to show through its light, creamy covering as spring draws near.

Because of these green cells in its bark, the outer covering of the quaking
aspen is more highly prized as a source of food by gnawing animals than the bark
of almost any other tree. The beaver is one creature that is strongly attracted

to aspen bark, both because of its soft and easy-to-chew texture and its nutrient value, which steadily increases as this season progresses. This is why a beaver that is able to regain its access to the shore through the thawing ice can be so easily lured to a spot supporting quaking aspen trees.

The varying hare is also well known for gnawing on the bark of the poplar during the late winter, especially if it has consumed most of the buds that were within its reach from the forest floor. The youngest twigs that are present throughout the crown of the aspen contain the bark that is most favorable to the hare. However, this section of the tree is only accessible to this ground dweller when it has been toppled to the ground by the strong winds that so frequently occur during March. Aspen saplings are also occasionally gnawed on by the hare, yet since these young trees develop only in open settings where cover is sparse, the hare is often reluctant to venture to those sites, where it would be more readily seen by its numerous natural enemies.

At this time of year, it takes several weeks for the flow of sap in the hardwood trees in the North Country to reach its peak, and trees don't completely fill their cells with a high concentration of liquid while cold winter weather remains. However, many of the processes which bring about the leaves of May have already been initiated, and their signs can be noted by the ever-so-slight change in the color of our deciduous woodlands.

Crusty Snow Season

The weather in the North Country during March typically oscillates between brief periods of spring-like warmth and blasts of air that originate over the Arctic, interspersed with a nor'easter or two and storms from the south that bring rain. As a result of the radical swings in temperature and the varying forms of precipitation, the snow during March often develops a crusty cover that impacts many wildlife populations.

A firm crust is of definite benefit to the mice and voles that live on the ground in forests and fields. During much of the winter, predators like the coyote and fox are able to locate these gnawing mammals by homing in on the faint sounds they generate while chewing, or when traveling over frozen leaves or dried grasses. When they detect the presence of such prey, these carnivores are well known for leaping directly onto the spot and quickly swiping aside the powder, or simply thrusting their snouts directly into the fluffy layer that covers the site in an attempt to snag their quarry. While this hunting tactic is often successful when the snow is soft, it becomes much less effective as a crust forms and thickens. If an icy layer develops and is hard enough to support the weight of a larger mammal, it is solid enough to serve as a barrier that prevents a fox or coyote from quickly accessing the environment beneath. While either of these predators can dig through any type of crust using their claws, its prey, upon hearing the scratching overhead, has an opportunity to begin its evasive maneuvers. These few extra seconds prior to an assault are often all a small rodent needs for it to reach a runway that quickly leads to a place of safety. Consequently, mice and voles are often able to move about with impunity from such attacks when a solid crust develops.

During times when the crust is hard enough to support their weight, predators may target the varying hare. With its enlarged, snowshoe-like feet, this creature

has a distinct advantage over all other quadrupeds when a deep layer of fluffy snow covers the swamps and conifer thickets that serve as its home. But a crust often allows a bobcat, fox, fisher, or coyote to run across the surface of the snow as fast as the varying hare, reducing its chances of eluding these natural enemies. Unfortunately for the hare, the absence of a crust has little impact on its ability to outmaneuver hawks or owls, which are also well known for preying on these small game animals.

For the grouse, a crust over the surface of the snow can be disastrous. During periods of intense cold, this ground-dwelling bird is known to dive head first into the snow at dusk in order to bury itself in the powder for the night. Since snow is an excellent insulating agent, a grouse can better retain its body heat during its period of inactivity if it is covered by a blanket of light, fluffy powder. On occasions when a crust forms during the afternoon, these birds have been known to plunge into this icy layer, resulting in a fatal neck injury. Naturalists have also reported that grouse can become trapped below a crust that formed overnight. A fast-moving cold front preceded by a period of freezing rain can create a layer of ice above a grouse that has burrowed into the snow for the night.

Crusty snow can be of benefit to several winter songbirds, as it allows seeds to more easily collect on the surface. The gales for which March is so infamous often shake loose the seeds in trees and shrubs that have been held in place since late the previous summer or autumn. A solid covering over the ground keeps these tiny fragments of food from sinking into the powder and disappearing from the sight of foraging birds.

It is difficult to predict how long the snow will last and what condition this white crystalline material will be in as winter transitions into spring. What we do know, however, is that until the start of the mud season, the condition of the surface of the snow will greatly impact the lives of many creatures which reside throughout our region.

Winterkill and Scavengers

As the snow pack gradually melts over the course of the first few weeks of spring, the wildlife casualties of the past season begin to appear and soon will start to thaw. Regardless of the adaptations an animal possesses for surviving the rigors of a North Country winter, sickness, old age, and inexperience coping with the hardships of a sub-arctic climate eventually take their toll. The depth of the snow, the intensity of the cold, and the unusual length of some bouts of bitter weather inevitably lead to a certain amount of the seasonal mortality often referred to as winterkill.

Yet, as tragic as these loses may seem, a reduction in the number of animals actually benefits the entire remaining wildlife community. When a population is reduced, individual animals experience less competition for food, denning or nesting sites, and living space. As a result, an animal that has established a claim to a particular piece of land will eventually be able to concentrate more of its time on finding food and engaging in activities associated with reproduction, rather than expending energy defending its ownership of that area against those animals that have been unable to locate a place of their own. Under some circumstances, a creature may actually be able to extend the boundaries of its territory without challenge, thereby increasing its access to food.

Winterkill is also a vital component of the diets of animals that scavenge. A coyote or fox, with its keen sense of smell, is able to easily locate the thawing carcasses of creatures ranging in size from deer and wild turkeys to squirrels and chickadees. Likewise, the ermine, marten, fisher, and skunk, in their springtime wanderings, will inevitably stumble upon the remains of some unfortunate victim of the winter and derive sustenance from it. Because a predator does not have to expend any energy chasing after a living individual or risk injury attacking an animal that is reluctant to serve as a meal, the frozen or partially thawed remains of a winter-killed creature is more beneficial to an animal's survival than a meal it must kill itself.

Animals like the raccoon and black bear, which are just beginning to shake off the grogginess of their winter's sleep, depend heavily on carrion to carry them through until the bounty of spring plants and bugs becomes available. A bear is well known for its ability to read the wind with its sensitive nose and follow the scent trail emanating from a carcass on which bacteria has just begun to act, and it has a digestive system that allows it to safely eat meat that is awash in bacteria. In this way the bear is able to acquire the protein it needs at this time of the year to replenish nutrients depleted during the months when it went without eating.

The raven, crow, and blue jay are also on the list of creatures that will eagerly feast on the remains of a deer, porcupine, coyote, or woodpecker that perished sometime over the past four months and was temporarily buried in nature's white blanket. Even chickadees have been observed making regular trips to a partially-eaten carcass of a winter-killed animal. This small white, gray, and black bird will glean the final shreds of meat from a skeleton, much as it will remove the last bits of suet from a strip placed near a bird feeder.

Those carcasses not located by a scavenger before they are completely thawed become the targets of a host of carrion-eating insects after they have been acted on for several weeks by the bacteria of decay. Various species of beetles, flies, and other invertebrates have evolved a sense of smell that effectively leads them to any rotting chunk of animal matter that exists on the forest floor.

Even the bones that are left after the scavengers and bugs finish with a carcass are gnawed on by a number of small creatures. Mice and voles have been observed chewing on these calcium-rich structures for the various minerals they contain.

It can be said that nothing in nature ever goes to waste, and any losses in the wildlife community during winter only go to ensure the success of those creatures that were able to survive this long and difficult period of time.

The Bald Eagle

For some birds, it is the complete disappearance of their food source, not the bitter cold, that drives them from northern New York as winter approaches. Generally, these avian creatures are quick to return to the North Country as soon as food becomes available again, regardless of prevailing weather conditions. The bald eagle is such a bird, as its reappearance into the Adirondacks coincides with the late winter opening of its favored hunting grounds.

It is ordinarily during the first week or two of March that a substantial thaw occurs across the region. This results in the runoff needed to create sizeable stretches of open water on the larger rivers that flow out of the mountains. It is along such ice-free waterways that the bald eagle searches for dead or live fish and other large aquatic animals. Because fish tend to confine their activities at this time of year to deep holes where the strength of the current is greatly reduced, the eagle concentrates most of its time scouring the shoreline for any fish

that has perished in the frigid and turbulent waters. Although occasionally a fish will venture near the surface and be detected by the keen eyes of the eagle, such prey are never easy to snag, especially in flowing water, so winter-killed ducks, muskrats, mink, and other forms of carrion seem to be the staple items in the eagle's diet. Occasionally, an eagle will discover a deer carcass or a dead coyote or fox. In such situations, this majestic raptor will repeatedly visit the remains until only bone and hair are left.

Along with the individuals that nest in this region, bald eagles that breed much further to the north are known to visit northern New York during March and the first half of April. According to biologists, the eagles that are seen before mid-April may either be ones that have a nesting territory nearby or transients that will be leaving in another several weeks.

Over the past several decades, numerous pairs of these impressive birds with the white head and tail feathers have taken up residence in the northern portion of New York. Like a Canada goose, the bald eagle forms a lifelong pair-bond with a single individual of the opposite sex. The pair constructs a very large nest of twigs near the top of a tall tree such as a towering white pine, and they will return to that nest every year as the mating season approaches. Even though it may remain completely intact from the previous year, the pair will add a collection of new sticks to this aerial platform prior to breeding. Since an eagle carrying a stick is a sure sign that the bird has a nest nearby, such sightings are of great value in locating these permanent nurseries.

During exceptionally mild winters, when large sections of Lake Champlain, the St. Lawrence River, and Lake Ontario fail to completely freeze, our resident eagles may simply travel to these ice-free settings to pass the winter. As long as open water exists and an adequate number of fish (dead or alive) can be taken from the surface, the eagles will remain despite periodic bouts of arctic weather.

The bald eagle may also take up winter residence along a section of highway that cuts through a deer wintering area where car-deer collisions are frequent. Some deer may be knocked over the snow bank by an impact with a car or truck, while other collision victims occasionally drag themselves into the woods a short distance before dying. Even though a fresh snowfall may cover a carcass, many are eventually sniffed out by a fox, coyote, or other flesh eater, and thereby exposed enough for an eagle to locate. Those deer that are killed instantly and left in the road are picked up eventually by a highway crew and deposited in certain designated places. It is quite common for several bald eagles to take up residence at such sites, especially if there is a consistent supply of road-killed animals deposited there.

As long as there is an adequate supply of fish or meat for this bird of prey to feed on, the bald eagle will brave the cold and avoid traveling to a more temperate climate. This symbol of our nation is an extremely hardy species that never fails to impress those individuals fortunate enough to see one close-up in the wilds.

Bluebird Box Time

Throughout the North Country, there are a number of birds that place their nests inside some type of protective enclosure. Among these cavity dwellers is the bluebird, which has experienced great difficulty over the past century finding a suitable place to locate its nest and then maintaining its hold on its selected nesting chamber. This situation has resulted in a substantial decline in its numbers all across its geographic range.

The eastern bluebird is New York's official state bird and at one time was a common resident of urban, suburban, and rural settings across the state. Since the early 1900s, however, this attractively-colored songster has experienced fierce competition for nesting cavities from two introduced species of birds.

Both the starling and house sparrow were brought to North America from Europe during the 1800s, and each has met with such ecological success that they are now among our most common birds. Like the bluebird, these birds locate their nests in a cavity, such as those inside a hollow tree, or in an appropriate-sized birdhouse. Yet, unlike the more timid bluebird, these two immigrants are aggressive when it comes to laying claim to a suitable nesting cavity.

Because of their larger bills, which are used as weapons when fighting other birds, and their more scrappy nature, both of these birds consistently win out in any dispute over a nesting site involving the bluebird. On occasions, the house sparrow has even been known to kill a bluebird that refuses to relinquish its hold on a particular cavity. All too often, the bluebird is left without a place to nest and fails to breed, leading to the serious reduction in its numbers.

Ornithologists unwilling to permit the demise of this handsome bird have discovered that it is possible to repopulate an area with bluebirds by allowing them to have undisputed access to a nesting cavity. This is done by putting out nesting boxes that are very specifically designed for bluebird occupancy in locations that are likely to be found by only bluebirds.

Because of its slightly smaller body size compared to a starling's, a bluebird is able to squeeze through an entrance that is exactly one and a half inches in diameter. As a result, if a box is constructed with a hole of this size, it will be passed over by any and all starlings that are in search of a place to build their

nests, leaving the box vacant for any bluebird in the area.

The house sparrow can be kept from finding a nest box by locating it at a site that is not commonly frequented by sparrows. Since this European bird is ordinarily attracted to areas around human dwellings, a nest box placed a fair distance from a house, barn, shed, or garage is not very likely to be taken over by a pair of such finches looking for shelter.

The bluebird is known to frequent open areas where the grass never gets too high and where the underbrush is not too dense. Places such as golf courses, pastures, fields adjacent to airport runways, or even large lawns are all equally attractive to this colorful perching bird. As a result, if you live in a fairly open area, especially where there is a spattering of trees nearby, a properly placed and well-designed bluebird house can be very beneficial to this native species.

Specific plans for building these specialized houses can be obtained from the North American Bluebird Society, the Department of Environmental Conservation, or the U.S. Fish and Wildlife Service. It is emphasized by the Bluebird Society that a poorly designed nest box may end up attracting both starlings and house sparrows, which would allow these birds to breed successfully in an area and further harm the chances of the bluebirds for making a comeback there.

There are times in March when the weather causes anyone with any sense to remain indoors. Building bluebird boxes is a rewarding way to spend an afternoon or evening when cold, rain, wind, or a combination of all three make it unfit for man, woman, or beast to venture outside. If you plan on engaging in such a project, it should be emphasized that these structures should be completed and put up outdoors before the end of March. Some experts believe that such a fabricated cavity should be exposed to the weather for a period of several weeks before the bluebirds' return from their wintering grounds. This gives the structure an opportunity to lose any human smells that may attract a mouse or other similar size critter that has been conditioned to associate people with food.

A Hard Time for Deer

By early March, it is not uncommon for nearly everyone, even ski enthusiasts and other snow lovers, to start wishing for the disappearance of the snow pack. But the desire in humans to see bare ground probably pales in comparison to any similar sentiment that a deer may experience, as snow causes this mammal more hardship than the cold.

Although the low temperatures that periodically develop in the Adirondacks do create hardship for the whitetail, its fur provides adequate protection against normal winter cold. In the autumn, a deer develops a coat of long, dense, hollow hair that is effective in allowing it to retain much of its body heat at temperatures above twenty below zero. (Air space that forms inside an animal's hair greatly increases its insulating value.) Consequently, it is only on nights when the mercury drops to arctic levels that deer experience difficulty in staying warm.

The relatively small, sharp hooves of the whitetail give it excellent traction on the mat of dead leaves and twigs that covers the forest floor, as well as on the loose soil and rocky surfaces that can occur in many settings. Its feet, however, are not well suited for effectively traversing snowy terrain; the deeper the snow gets, the harder it becomes for the whitetail to trudge through the powder. Any snow depth greater than a foot forces a deer to continually retrace its steps when going between two locations. A deer will also follow the tracks made by another deer rather than break a new trail. Within a few days after a heavy snowfall, well trodden paths known as runways begin to form. These thoroughfares provide a deer with relatively easy avenues to travel; however, the snow conditions that allow for such paths greatly restrict the sites the whitetail can visit.

As snow depth increases to two feet or more, the freedom of this mammal to move about in search of food becomes further restricted. In some cases, a deer may be unable to access the shrubs and small trees upon which it depends for food, even though they may only be a few dozen yards from a runway.

Because deer develop a layer of fat during the summer and autumn, most are able to tolerate a period of a few weeks to a month of restricted feeding. Should

the snow depth remain less than a foot throughout the winter, most whitetails can survive this period of famine.

The return of warmer weather in March brings with it a corresponding return of atmospheric moisture which can translate into greater snowfalls during this month. While the western Adirondack region develops most of its snow pack from lake effect storms, eastern sections are prone to nor'easters which can dump copious amounts of snow in March. Late season blizzards are especially hard on deer that have been weakened by the long winter. A fifteen inch dump of heavy snow in March is more disastrous to the whitetail than a similar accumulation of drier powder in early January.

The crust that frequently forms in March creates added hardship. Since a deer's hooves can punch through the surface layer, its legs will quickly sink into the holes in the crust, further impeding its ability to move. This is the time when a coyote can easily catch and bring down a whitetail. There are stories from a century ago of trappers on snowshoes who would run down deer when such crusty snow conditions formed in order to boast of killing one with only a knife. A large domestic dog or a pack of smaller dogs are also known to attack and kill deer during March when the snow is deep and a crust has formed. This is why the DEC encourages dog owners to keep their pets from roaming into areas inhabited by deer during March.

Conditions during March can vary greatly. There are some years when only a minimal amount of snow falls during this month and periodic thaws reduce previous accumulations to manageable depths. Deer usually flourish when spring comes early. During years when repeated nor'easters and other snow events add to the depth of the snow pack, or when a crust forms and remains for an unusually long period of time, it is the predators and scavengers that make out the best.

Breeding Time for Mice

In nature, some events that signal the onset of spring are quite conspicuous, while others are exceedingly subtle and totally overlooked. The start of the breeding season for mice is one occasion that goes completely unnoticed by humans, yet its significance in the natural world should never be underestimated.

Few mammals are as ubiquitous in the Adirondacks, along with most other environments across the country, as are mice. These prolific rodents abound in a wide variety of settings, particularly in the vast expanses of forests and semi-wooded thickets that cover so much of northern New York. Because of their relative abundance and appealing taste (assuming you are a wild-meat eater), mice are the number one target of nearly every predator of this region, regardless of size. The coyote is just as likely to spend time stalking a mouse as an ermine or a short-tailed shrew. Mice are also frequently attacked from the air by owls and hawks and have been reported to be taken on occasion by great blue herons, snakes, pike, bass, and other creatures.

This constant predation on mice causes them to experience the highest rate of mortality among the mammals of our region. The only way they can survive as a species is by maintaining an equally high rate of reproduction to compensate for their losses. Since all of their energy and resources are spent on dealing with the

harshness of the climate and the shortages of food that develop once the snow is on the ground, mice are not afforded the luxury of being able to reproduce from mid-November through February.

As conditions for survival begin to improve in March, the breeding urge is reawakened. Individuals that were born in the autumn may have passed the winter in the nest of their parents. In this way they may share the body heat of an adult or two and have access to the caches of food formed by a parent during the summer and autumn. With the approach of the breeding season, these now-mature individuals are forced out. The distance that a young mouse has to travel to find a territory of its own and a mate to share it with varies greatly. If predation in the immediate area is average to above normal, a mouse may not have to venture very far before encountering an unoccupied section of the forest floor.

At a time when only a limited supply of food may be available, the normally three-week gestation period can be extended to a full month. By early to mid-April, female mice will be giving birth to their first litter of the season. The male is known to regularly assist in the rearing of the four to six babies that typically make up the first litter. It is not long after giving birth that the female mates again. In this way she is ready to produce her second litter by the time her first is nearing the stage in their development when they are able to go out on their own. This process of repeat reproduction will continue throughout the summer, enabling a single pair of mice to have up to five litters a year, provided that neither adult is picked off by a predator.

Mortality among young mice after they leave the nest is especially high, as they are inexperienced at concealing their presence from natural enemies and eluding capture once detected. Those individuals from the first and second litters that were able to avoid being eaten are usually able to breed before the end of the season, since mice become sexually mature by the time they are two months old. This further adds to the mouse population.

It is during the late spring and early summer when young mice are exploring their surroundings that young predators are starting to develop their skills at detecting, stalking, and attacking prey. Without the swelling numbers of mice, nearly all of these animals would fail to find a meal.

While mice are a nuisance when they become regular visitors to your cupboards or pantry, they are a vital link in the food chain. And it is normally in late March that they become part of the process that will benefit those many forms of wildlife that are held in greater esteem by the general public.

Snow Pool Mosquitoes

Rain, warm wind, and sun are all responsible for the disappearance of the snow pack, which raises the level of the rivers and lakes, causes basement flooding, and triggers the long process of development in many North Country mosquitoes.

In northern regions, the bulk of the mosquito population passes the winter in the form of fertilized eggs. These tiny, dormant structures are placed during the summer in a dry depression that typically floods at this time of year. As they become immersed in near-freezing water, these enclosed entities awaken and start their transformation into larvae. It often takes from several weeks up to a month, depending on the water temperature, for the eggs to hatch and the miniature, caterpillar-like creatures, known to some as wigglers, to emerge. By this time, these seasonal puddles have warmed and become laden with an array of suspended organic particles and other forms of nutrient-enriched matter on which the larvae feed. Along with the virtual smorgasbord of food, small, temporary bodies of water tend to be devoid of the larger predatory organisms which frequent more permanent aquatic settings. This absence of natural enemies allows the larvae to develop without a great reduction in their numbers.

As drier conditions begin to prevail in May and warmer weather promotes evaporation, mosquito nurseries shrink and start to disappear. At this point the vast majority of larvae have transformed into the pupa stage and can survive out of water. After experiencing their final bodily reorganization, the adults appear when spring is transitioning into summer. It takes only a few days for adults of the opposite sex to come together and breed. The fertilized females then turn their attention to finding the meal of blood that is required for the cluster of eggs within them to properly form.

Unlike mosquitoes that exist in far more temperate and tropical regions, many northern species do not seek out stagnant pools of water in which to lay their egg masses. Instead, these insects, known as snowpool mosquitoes, seek out depressions that tend to remain dry until the end of winter. During the autumn, the egg masses may get covered with a protective layer of dead leaves and in winter, with a blanket of snow. Because they're dry, the eggs are safeguarded from the damage that would occur by expanding ice crystals when water freezes. It is in this form that the mosquitoes in this geographic region have the best chances for surviving to the next spring. However, should these depressions become flooded by a torrential rain after the eggs have been deposited there, certain chemical and thermal signals prevent the eggs from beginning development prematurely.

Most snowpool mosquitoes in the North Country have been shown to be univoltine, which means they lay only a single set of eggs during the course of their lives; therefore, the female only takes one blood meal. Any harmful organisms which are ingested by this type of female mosquito are either digested by her or perish within her body when she eventually dies later in the summer. These species never have the opportunity to introduce ingested pathogens into the body of another organism.

Although not as abundant during the spring, there are numerous other varieties of mosquitoes that inhabit the North Country. Many of these employ far different strategies for surviving the winter, and most of these are multivoltine, which means that the female is capable of breeding more than once during the summer. It is these types of mosquitoes which are responsible for the transmission of disease. After taking blood from one host and laying a set of eggs, the female will seek out another animal from which to draw a meal. In the process, pathogens acquired during an earlier contact may be introduced to the second or third host through a blood vessel. Since several of these species overwinter as adults, any mosquito seen before mid-May is not likely to be a snowpool mosquito, and should be regarded as a vector of disease.

As the ground becomes saturated by melting snow during the next several weeks, and puddles begin to form where they typically do each year at this time, the process of mosquito development begins, eventually reaching its climax on peaceful, early-summer evenings.

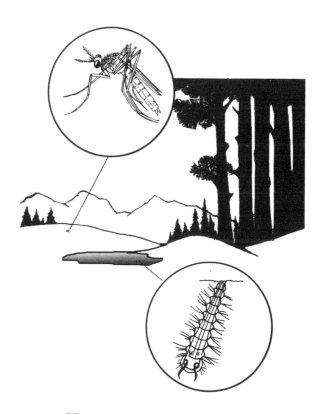

Denning Time for the Fox and Coyote

As periods of spring-like weather become more frequent and prolonged, our region's two most common canines, the red fox and coyote, begin to prepare the dens that will soon be used to house their new families. In the Adirondacks, it is usually during late March or early April when these members of the dog clan give birth to their annual litter, and a den is essential to protect the pups from natural enemies and occasional bouts of inclement weather. (While both of these predators sit atop the food chain in our region, their pups are still fair game to a fisher, bobcat, or large hawk.)

Despite the severity of a North Country winter, neither the fox nor coyote retreats into any type of protective enclosure to escape the cold. On blustery occasions, both are known to seek out densely wooded places that are sheltered from the wind. However, in such areas, these animals always rest in the open and never venture into any form of cubby, cave, or burrow that would afford some relief from the arctic air.

As new life starts to stir within the female, the urge to locate a den arises and the search for an appropriate site begins. For older animals, dens that were used during preceding years are revisited and assessed for possible occupancy. First time residents of an area may rely on one or more of the dens used by their territory's previous owners. These shelters were undoubtedly stumbled upon earlier in the season while the animal was hunting for prey or exploring the territory, and their locations seem to be well remembered.

If none of the former sites are acceptable to the female, the search continues. While both of these canines strongly prefer to make their dens in the ground, some individuals may elect to set up housekeeping within a suitable hollow log that is situated in a favorite spot.

Since neither of these animals is well adapted for excavating an entire subterranean complex from scratch, most rely on a burrow system that has been previously dug by either a woodchuck or skunk. While the tunnels and chambers created by these smaller critters are far too small for a fox, let alone a coyote, both canines are able to scrape the walls of their passageways and interior earthen rooms to create additional space.

While it may seem that the frost in the soil would prevent any modification to a den at this time of year, most dens are located in areas that are dry enough to allow for such enlargement. Establishing a den in a well-drained site is essential, otherwise, water will seep into the living chamber during periods of heavy spring rain and snow melt.

As a rule, a den has at least two entrances and often extends two to four feet below the surface, allowing an animal to utilize the natural warmth of the ground and limit the amount of cold air that can sink in. This provides an interior envi-

ronment that is more favorable to the infants when they are born.

As spring progresses, both the red fox and the coyote may relocate their babies to a new den in a slightly different area. Additional moves may also occur periodically throughout the spring and early summer. According to wildlife researchers, it is not uncommon for these mammals to have as many as six different dens or nest sites that are occupied for only a few weeks at a time. This helps prevent the den from becoming infested with skin parasites such as fleas, ticks, and lice.

By late July, the developing pups have reached a size and level of strength that makes them unlikely targets for any large predator. This eliminates the need to retreat into a den when it comes time to rest. From that point on, foxes and coyotes will remain outside until very early the next spring, when a new litter is about to be born and a den is again needed by the pair.

The Rabbit vs. The Hare

The creature normally associated with the Easter season is the rabbit; however, in the Adirondacks, the symbol of this early springtime holiday should be the hare. While it is widely believed that these creatures are one and the same, there are definite differences between these two forms of wildlife.

As a rule, rabbits construct a nest for housing their babies, whereas hares do not. After breeding in the early spring, the female rabbit usually seeks out a sheltered spot and excavates a sizeable depression in the soil. Occasionally, she may select a hollow log or an abandoned woodchuck or skunk burrow to serve as a nesting site if one is readily available in a protected location. After settling into its retreat, the rabbit assembles a mass of dried grasses, weeds, moss, and other soft material to serve as bedding.

The female hare fails to make any similar preparations for the birth of her babies. While she will seek out a sheltered spot in which to bear her litter, she never constructs an elaborate nest. Because baby hares lack the protection afforded by a nest, nature compensates by providing them with a full coat of fur at the time of their birth, whereas a rabbit is essentially naked when it is born, and its eyes do not open until it is at least a week old. Young hares are far more precocious, for not only are they able to see, but infant hares are also able to move about and even run for a short distance within a day or two after being born. Young rabbits do not leave their nest until they are at least two full weeks old.

The sole species of hare that exists in the North Country is the varying hare. While also referred to as the snowshoe rabbit because of its enlarged feet, this animal is very much a hare. The cottontail rabbit, which is found to a limited extent in warmer valley settings in and around the Adirondack Park, has smaller feet in comparison to the hare and lacks the ability to bound across a snowy landscape. A hare's hind legs are also slightly larger in proportion to its body size than a rabbit's are. As a result, the hare is faster and can maneuver more easily than its distant cousin.

The varying hare is so named because of the way its fur changes color from grayish brown in summer to white in winter. While the cottontail experiences a slight color change from one season to another, it pales in comparison to the change the hare undergoes.

The varying hare and the cottontail rabbit also prefer to inhabit different ecological settings. Our hare thrives in dense conifer forests, especially those around lowland swamps and at upper elevations just below the tree line. Alder thickets and mixed woodlands where clusters of young evergreens completely cover the forest floor are also commonly inhabited by the snowshoe.

cottontail rabbit

snowshoe hare

The cottontail prefers semi-open, brush-covered areas or the edges of hardwoods that border apple orchards, corn fields, or large gardens. Since the varying hare is a denizen of the Great North Woods, its diet is mainly composed of woody matter such as the buds and bark of certain small trees and shrubs. The cottontail strongly favors non-woody food sources, such as grasses, the stalks of certain weeds, berries, fruits that have fallen to the ground, and of course, items from the garden. During the winter the cottontail may be forced to eat tree buds; however, it will quickly change back to herbaceous matter when such items become available.

In recent years, the population of cottontails in and around the Adirondacks appears to be increasing. Milder winters with less snow are highly favorable to this mammal. Additionally, human encroachment into heavily-forested areas has produced more openings in the woods and a resultant increase in the plants that the cottontail finds to its liking. Yet despite the cottontails' growing numbers, the varying hare is still the Adirondacks' number one "rabbit."

On a Sunday morning during the early spring, a mythological creature will be visiting area homes to place chocolate eggs and jelly beans in baskets lined with plastic grass. Although known as the Easter rabbit, the bunny-like critter responsible for this action in the North Country is really the Easter hare.

The Otter in Spring

Ice-out time in the Adirondacks is a welcome occasion for lakefront property owners, boating enthusiasts, and the many forms of wildlife whose lives are so intricately tied to our larger bodies of water. One aquatic creature that finds its range rapidly expanding when open water replaces a sheet of ice is the otter, a seldom-seen member of the weasel family that is widely distributed across the North Country.

During the winter, the otter confines most of its activities to rivers and streams. It is also known to periodically venture into those sections of lakes and ponds where water rich in dissolved oxygen flows into these otherwise ice-sealed aquatic settings. Throughout the winter, this sleek, webbed-footed creature forages along the bottom, probing nooks and crannies and occasionally overturning submerged organic debris in its attempt to uncover the small animals, fish, and invertebrates upon which it feeds.

From late summer through mid-winter, the otter retreats into any type of shelter that it comes across when it feels the need to rest. During March or very early April, as the female nears the time when she will give birth, she instinctively seeks out a place that affords far better protection. Higher ground which is less prone to the flooding that typically accompanies spring in the Adirondacks is strongly preferred. Additionally, an otter attempts to place its nursery in a location that is not likely to be stumbled upon by a meandering coyote or bobcat that may prey on the helpless otter kits.

Like several other members of the weasel family, the female otter breeds within a week or two after giving birth, then enters a gestation period of nearly one full year. As the female comes into heat, her scent is quick to draw the attention of male otters. Ordinarily, her reproductive partner is the male whose range overlaps with hers. However, since many males are on the move at this time during the spring, especially those that have no female residing close by, a female

may encounter several suitors. If a resident male encounters a rival encroaching onto his domain, he is quick to attack. Although the otter is seen as the most social and fun-loving member of the weasel family, its playful temperament never extends to other males during this period of spring. Since male otters are also known to attack and kill very young babies, the female is extremely careful not to let any male come too close to her den until much later in the season.

The helpless state of the otter kits in the weeks immediately after birth and their slow rate of development allow the female to leave her babies unattended for several hours after nursing them without having them wander out of the den. It is not until the kits are five weeks old that their eyes open, and it's another week before they begin to regularly interact with both their litter mates and their mother. At eight weeks, the kits frequently appear at the entrance of their den, yet they do not venture out until at least a week or two later. By then it is early to mid-June, and the water is finally at a temperature that is favorable for their first dip. It doesn't take long for otter kits to learn to swim, although it is not until the end of the summer that they have mastered the skill of rapidly maneuvering through their aquatic habitat. At the same time as they are being introduced to the water, their mother gradually weans them off her milk, and the young otters begin developing their appetite for the small animals, fish, and invertebrates that they will consume for the rest of their lives.

As lakes open up across the region, only lone otters can be seen in a cove or bay during the early morning or evening hours. It will be at least another month and a half or more before a playful group may be noticed frolicking in the water, careening down a mud slide along the shore, or simply gracing our lakes as only the otter can do.

Beavers on the Move

Several weeks after the ice breaks up on lakes, ponds, and marshes across the Adirondacks, there is also a break-up of the beaver families that occupy these same bodies of water. The beaver is a rather social creature and normally lives in a colony composed of an adult female and male, along with the young from their two previous years. As the time draws near in mid-spring for the matriarch of the colony to bear her annual litter, the younger members of the colony begin to travel in different directions, with some leaving the area entirely, and others venturing into more remote places within the boundaries of the individual colony.

During the winter, the presence of a solid covering of ice over the beaver's world greatly limits its ability to stray very far from the lodge it uses during this season. With the thawing of the ice, the beaver becomes free to move about the colony's territory and once again gain access to the shore, where it forages for certain woody plants. In winter, a beaver feeds entirely on the bark of twigs and branches which were cached in a submerged pile just outside the underwater entrance to its lodge. By the time the ice thaws, the trees and shrubs near the water's edge experience a return of nutrient-enriched sap which flows mainly through the bark. The change in a beaver's diet from waterlogged scraps of food

to fresh bark boosts its nutritional intake and helps push the individuals nearing their second birthday toward physical maturity.

As they gain in size and strength, the older juveniles begin to experience an urge to establish a territory of their own and form a pair bond with another individual. It is during mid-April through May that the maturing two year old beaver finally departs its family's pond. Travel almost always occurs in the water, as the beaver's large, webbed hind feet make it slow and awkward on land. However, this creature may be forced to periodically cross dry ground in its search to find a suitable aquatic setting.

In areas where the beaver population is near saturation level, a maturing adult may immediately encounter a neighbor just beyond the boundaries of its parent's territory that is unwilling to tolerate the presence of trespassers. Under such conditions, a young beaver may decide to return home and refuse to leave. In some cases, the adult female is known to attack her offspring in an attempt to drive them out and prevent then from returning.

A beaver in search of a home may have to travel long distances and explore numerous aquatic settings. When all favorable locations are already claimed, a beaver may be forced to take up residence in a less than desirable location. Swamps that are surrounded by conifer forests, large drainage ditches along the side of highways, or fast-moving mountain streams that run through beech, maple, and yellow birch forests are considered marginal at best.

Once a two year old finds an unoccupied section of lake, marsh, or stream, it will claim its ownership by placing scent mounds at entrance points. In places where there is a current, the beaver will also begin to erect a dam to elevate the water level and enlarge the area in which it can swim. Any town highway crew member can attest to the beaver's drive to build a dam, both in the mid to late spring when it's on the move and again in the late summer and autumn when preparations begin for winter.

As the female nears the time for her to give birth, she may become hostile toward her mate. This causes him to leave the lodge and take up residence in one of the many temporary shelters that a family of beavers creates around its territory. Occasionally, a few of the yearlings may join the male, or they may venture on their own to explore the far reaches of their parents' domain. Even the adult female may relocate her den into an auxiliary lodge prior to giving birth, as the dwelling occupied during the winter is often abandoned shortly after the break-up of the ice.

It is usually not until early to mid-summer, after the newborn kits have been introduced to the water and are beginning to eat vegetation on their own, that a beaver family comes back together. But in April, families are just beginning to disperse and establish a warm-weather routine that tends to keep them apart until their preparations for the winter must begin again.

Brook Trout in Spring

In the streams and small rivers that so abundantly flow throughout the North Country, the brook trout emerges from its sedate winter routine sometime in April to become the nemesis of aquatic invertebrates and the target of early season anglers.

Even though the brook trout thrives in the frigid waters of northern streams, this cold-blooded creature has difficulty generating the energy necessary to contend with the current when the temperature is within a degree or two of freezing. In such cold water, this fish spends all of its time in places where the strength of the current is minimal. A deep hole or an eddy just behind a boulder or a sunken log offers a microhabitat that is highly favorable to the brook trout. In such a spot, a fish can spend the winter without expending much effort. Throughout this time, the brook trout sinks into a rather lethargic state and feeds only when edible

items settle in the water nearby.

As the sun increases in intensity during April, water temperatures begin to rise ever so slowly to more favorable levels for this colorful trout. Even though stream conditions still numb an angler's legs through insulated waders, brook trout begin to respond to the slight warming and become more active and lively as the end of the month nears.

Since the strength of the current can be quite formidable from the runoff of melting snow, a trout does not expend much energy fighting the force of the onrushing water at this time of year. Rather, it typically remains poised at the very edge of its hole or eddy and carefully watches for pieces of edible matter approaching in the current, then darts in and gulps them down. Like most fish, the brook trout depends almost entirely on its eyesight to detect an approaching bit of food.

During times of high water, it is quite common for the current to loosen submerged rocks and other sunken items that shelter the array of invertebrates which pass the winter season in such settings. Consequently, there is ordinarily an ample supply of mayfly and stonefly nymphs in swollen streams, along with numerous other types of immature insects bouncing over the bottom as they are swept downstream.

Wet flies are lures that have been designed to most closely resemble the aquatic stage of various bugs during the colder months of the year. As a result, the chances of successfully landing one of these feisty fish during the early part of trout season are better when using some type of wet fly rather than other categories of artificial lures.

Small worms or pieces of these annelids also seem to work well in attracting the attention of a feeding trout, although normally the earthworm does not occur in streams and is not a common component of a trout's diet. It is believed that earthworms simulate the appearance of other lower forms of animal matter that have been torn from their resting spots by the action of the rapidly flowing water.

Anglers who want to be successful in streams during April and early May must not only use the appropriate bait, but also keep it as close to the bottom as possible. When not at the edge of an eddy, the brook trout spends an inordinate amount of time cruising along the bottom, where the current is reduced. There it is also more likely to locate a bug, or a morsel of food trapped between two stones. Getting entangled in a submerged snag is perhaps the biggest dilemma that confronts a stream fisherman in spring, along with tolerating the intense cold that can permeate one's entire body. This is in addition, of course, to convincing a spouse to permit a fishing excursion in lieu of raking the lawn or doing one of the dozens of other outdoor chores that should be completed before the start of bug season.

The Snipe

As a means of engaging in humor, some novice naturalists, boy scouts, and fun-loving sportsmen may bring up the topic of the snipe. Discussions typically center on the various methods and techniques for spotting one of these elusive feathered creatures and the innovative practices (based on pure nonsense) for hunting it. However, few of these individuals know that the snipe is a real bird, not just a fictitious creature created solely to tease gullible people.

Appropriately classified as a shore bird, the snipe spends nearly all of its time among the lush plant life that covers those areas where dry land transitions into water. Fresh water marshes, large wet meadows, weedy thickets that form along the shores of shallow ponds, and the backwaters of rivers are all haunts of this common bird.

Because of its preference for feeding and resting in patches of dense vegetation, the snipe is extremely difficult to spot, and its mottled brown plumage, designed to blend in perfectly with the dried grasses that are always around it, makes a chance sighting even less likely.

Because of its resemblance to the woodcock, another resident of semi-aquatic settings, the snipe can be mistaken for this close relative on those rare occasions when it is spotted. Although these birds are nearly the same size and possess distinctively long and slender bills, there are several ways to distinguish between the two. The snipe has a slightly leaner build compared to the more robust woodcock, and the neck and legs of the snipe are longer. Also, the mottled coloring of a snipe's plumage is grayer compared to the more orange hue of a woodcock's feathers.

The definitive means of telling a snipe from a woodcock is by the pattern of stripes on the top of its head. The woodcock bears bands that extend from side to side, while the snipe possesses a set of stripes that run from the front to the back of its head. However, since it is not easy to clearly see this pattern, ornithologists typically rely on its leaner profile and more lanky body shape to identify a snipe from a distance.

Because of its dependence on soil invertebrates for food, the snipe does not migrate to its northern nesting areas until at least the middle of April. It is not

until the ground thaws and a resurgence of life occurs in the soil that the snipe returns in the spring.

As with many other common birds of the North Country, the presence of the snipe is regularly confirmed by the unique call produced by the male throughout the spring and early summer. Shortly after it returns to a suitable area, the male attempts to establish and maintain its hold on a territory by producing a breeding song. This eerie sound also draws the attention of any female snipe in the area, along with any uninformed human who will immediately wonder what the heck is making that noise.

Rather than perch in a prominent spot and bellow out a melodious song, the snipe, like the woodcock, engages in a flight ritual that results in its hallmark sound. However, unlike the aerial display of the woodcock, which occurs only during the twilight hours following sunset and preceding sunrise, a snipe's courtship flight may be carried out any time during the day.

As a rule, the male snipe flies in a wide circle around the area, typically remaining well above the tops of trees and shrubs. At various points in its flight, it rapidly dives while pushing its tail feathers out at an angle that exposes them to the passing air. The rushing air causes the feathers to resonate, yielding a series of very brief, hooting-whistle notes that increase in pitch and decrease in volume over a span of three to four seconds. This "wah-wah-wah-wah-wah-wah" call has a haunting tone unlike the sound made by any other bird. Since the snipe is not large, and it performs this display at a considerable height, it is rarely seen when making this call, which only adds to its eerie quality.

Among the more serious bird watchers of the North Country, the snipe is not a joke designed to lead individuals who want to learn something about the environment astray. They know it is a very real, rarely-seen bird with a springtime call that is sure to be a noteworthy occurrence on a trip to the wet, marshy settings in which it resides.

The Turkey Vulture

The odor given off by the rapidly decaying remains of an animal that perished over the winter can be quite offensive to anyone who should happen to come downwind of one. However, the smell of a decomposing carcass is very appealing to the turkey vulture, one of nature's most effective scavengers.

It is ordinarily during April when these large black birds begin to reappear in the skies over the North Country. Like other raptors, the turkey vulture is well designed for soaring, and it is almost always seen riding thermals in its seemingly effortless style of flight. Because it holds its wings above the level of its body, forming a slightly V-shaped profile (as opposed to a hawk, which holds its wings outstretched or in line with its body), a soaring vulture can be easily recognized from a distance.

While riding air currents, a turkey vulture is ever alert to the sights and smells of dead animals. Like other birds of prey, it has a well-developed set of

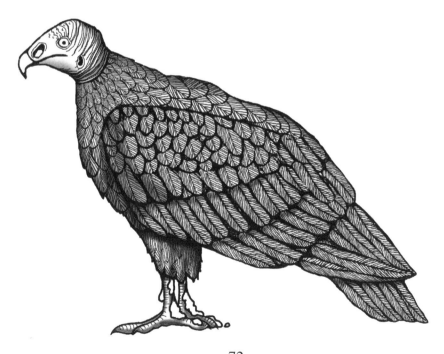

eyes that allows it to detect a potential meal from a fair distance away. But it is smell, rather than sight, that seems to be the main factor that draws a vulture to a source of food. Unlike other birds, the vulture has an exceptionally keen sense of smell. As a result, one of these gliding scavengers will readily detect the foul aroma of a putrefying chunk of carrion and follow it back to the source. To test the effectiveness of this bird's olfactory sense, researchers have put out sizeable animal carcasses and completely covered them with various materials such as soil, dead leaves, and other debris from the forest floor. In all cases, the vultures were eventually able to locate these buried caches of food, despite the total lack of visual cues.

While rotting meat eventually becomes awash with bacteria and other organisms that are harmful to most creatures, the turkey vulture has a digestive system that is able to tolerate such matter without experiencing any ill effects. Consequently, this bird is often responsible for ridding the environment of items that are too far along in a state of decay for many other scavengers to consume.

Following a typical Adirondack winter, there is seldom a shortage of food to greet returning turkey vultures. After a mild winter, however, the situation can be quite different. Mortality among many wildlife populations, especially deer, may be significantly lower when mild temperatures and limited snowfall prevail throughout the winter. During these years, the turkey vulture may experience great difficulty locating a meal upon its return to the region.

In another month or so, when winter killed carcasses decompose beyond the point at which a vulture will pick at the remains, or during years when there weren't many in the first place, the attention of this bird shifts to road kill. After the first few periods of really warm weather, the vulture may be regularly seen soaring above the highways that crisscross the region. Because of the efficiency of its flight, a vulture is able to survey many miles of road in search of creatures that lie dead on or near the pavement.

It does not take long during the latter part of spring and in the summer for this road kill to putrefy. Upon reaching that stage at which a smell foul enough to repulse most scavengers permeates the air, the vulture will likely take note and begin its job of ridding the environment of matter which few other creatures will go near.

Water Striders

It is nearly impossible to detect the gradual resurgence of invertebrate activity in streams, rivers, ponds, and marshes during the spring. Upon emerging from their winter dormancy, nearly all of the many insects and other bugs associated with the water stay very near the bottom until later in the season. Only the water strider may be regularly noted during this time, as its life on the surface of nearly any body of fresh water puts it in plain view.

The water strider is one of only a few insects that are uniquely adapted for using the surface of the water as a platform for hunting prey. During water's liquid phase, it develops an ultra thin surface layer of resistance caused by the electrical nature of its molecules. Known as surface tension, this property of water is able to provide a weak uplifting force which can counter the pull of gravity on lightweight objects and temporarily keep them afloat until they inevitably tear or break this delicate layer and sink. Even pollen grains, which can be nearly microscopic in size, eventually resist the surface tension and drop to the bottom.

The water strider possesses elongated feet that lie flat on the surface, rather than poke downward through it, and its feet are covered with special hair-like cells that repel water and fail to disrupt the surface tension, even though tiny depressions of the surface film may be noted under its feet, especially if light conditions are favorable. In addition to providing support, the feet of a water strider enable it to move easily across the surface. Rather than provide traction like a bottom of a sneaker or a vibrum sole of a boot, the hairs covering its feet function more like the blades of an ice skate, enabling it to glide over the water when it pushes its legs outward.

Since detergents dissolve surface tension, the water strider finds it impossible to function in areas where these chemicals have been released into the water. Only a drop or two of detergent in a lake will cause a nearby water strider to break through the surface and sink to the bottom like other organisms do. If it is unable to find a stick or a stalk of a plant upon which it can climb back out into the air, this bug will eventually drown.

Unlike most insects, the water strider uses only its long, thread-like middle and hind sets of legs for motion, giving it an appearance which prevents it from being mistaken for any other type of invertebrate. The front set of legs is much smaller and functions more like arms; they are usually kept folded near its head and are adapted for grabbing small organisms that have either fallen onto the surface or are swimming just below it.

The water strider is able to sense the minute vibrations on the surface produced by a bug that has accidentally dropped into the water and is thrashing about in an attempt to move. Once it detects these signals, it zeroes in on the point of origin and attacks the victim before it breaks the surface tension and becomes a meal for a creature that preys on submerged invertebrates.

Like a spider, a water strider injects its prey with a solution of potent digestive enzymes. These chemicals act on the various organic molecules composing the body of the victim and break them down into a nutrient broth. After a period of time, the water strider will suck in the newly-formed slurry of protein and fat, which will be quickly assimilated into its own system.

Because it is so small, the water strider does not pose any danger to humans. Its bite can barely be felt, and it would never attempt to attack a person unless that individual decided to grab hold of it.

During mid-spring, as the water begins to warm, most invertebrates connected to the water return to an active state. The first of these to be seen is the small-bodied bug with the four long legs that allow it to skim across the surface, an ecological setting that few other organisms can exist on for any length of time.

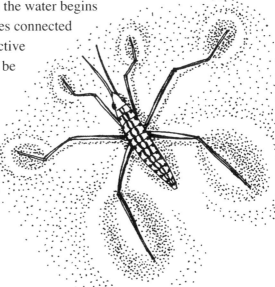

May

Spring Changes in the Whitetail

It is ordinarily during the first week of May when the North Country starts to become noticeably greener with each passing day. In response to the rapid eruption of leafy vegetation, deer experience some subtle yet definite changes in their digestive system in order to accommodate these new food sources.

Unlike humans and most other mammals, a deer depends mainly on microorganisms, not digestive enzymes, to chemically act on its food and convert it into a form that can be utilized by its system. The strains of protozoa which develop within its digestive tract are quite simple and are unable to act on more than one or two specific types of plants. Consequently, once this animal starts to focus its feeding attention on a selected source of food, the microorganisms that are designed for rendering nutrients from these items gradually become entrenched in its system. This allows a deer to take advantage of that specific food source and virtually nothing else.

From the time that the leaves drop during the autumn until early spring, there are only a few items for a deer to eat in this geographic setting. The upper roots of selected herbaceous plants such as wood ferns, the scale-like leaves of cedar, and the end buds of certain species of deciduous trees and shrubs become the deer's sole source of nourishment.

When sprouting foliage starts to cloak the region in green, there is a resurgence of items for this herbivore to feast upon. As increasingly greater quantities of greens are ingested by a whitetail, new cultures of protozoa are formed to take advantage of these enriched sources of food. The microorganisms that were critical to the survival of the deer only a few weeks earlier are now reduced in concentration and eventually become dormant until that time in the autumn when woody browse must again be ingested for nourishment.

The change in a deer's diet to tender and more nutritious items allows this hoofed creature to begin the long process of replenishing its depleted energy reserves, including fat. All too often, after its fat reserves are totally depleted, the whitetail is forced to burn other body tissues to remain alive during a North Country winter. It is during the spring when the intake of more nutritious food

items begins to rebuild both fat and muscle in the deer.

Since emerging leaves and new shoots are rich in a variety of basic elements, including calcium, this intake also helps to stimulate the formation and sustain the development of a buck's antlers. In a northern climate, most bucks typically shed their antlers during the very end of December or early in January, leaving them without any attractive boney headwear for the first four months of the year.

Eventually, knob-like swellings form on top of each side of a buck's head. These nubs are firmly attached to the skull and serve as the base of its new rack. A layer of velvety skin containing a multitude of blood vessels forms a covering over the rapidly-developing antlers. As blood flows to this area, calcium compounds are removed and turned into dense, bone-like deposits that add to the length, width, and shape of the emerging spikes.

As a general rule, the older bucks grow a larger rack than younger individuals. Since older animals have learned where the richest sources of food exist, they are more inclined to consume items that will result in the more sizeable set of antlers, along with an improved state of health. Scientists have also discovered that genetics plays a role in the size of a deer's antlers and the number of points that eventually form on them. It is believed that a buck with a system which can effectively extract and utilize calcium will likely pass this physiological ability on to its offspring.

Over the course of the next several weeks, a deer will also change color. As warmer weather becomes the rule, the whitetail gradually sheds its thick coat of dense, dark-colored hair. This coat is ideally adapted for keeping a deer warm in winter, as well as with helping to conceal it during a period when the nights are long and the days tend to be mostly grey and overcast. Replacing this layer of fur is a thin, rusty-tan summer coat which more effectively allows a deer to dissipate body heat and blend in with a much brighter background of greater light intensity.

The return of green to the North Country landscape during May brings with it many changes, some of which occur in the region's best known plant eater.

Graceful Flying Swallows

While all birds that inhabit the North Country are capable of flight, true mastery of this skill belongs to the swallows. With their graceful gliding turns and dives, swallows appear more elegant when moving through the air than almost any other flying creature. So unique is their strong yet smooth, flowing style of flight that it may be used to identify them.

Aside from adding beauty to the sky, the flight of the swallows is designed to help them snatch insects from the air. When they see a bug, these birds quickly redirect their flight in an attempt to catch it in their mouths. Although swallows do not have an unusually large bill, their mouth opens wide enough to allow them to swallow an insect which is on the wing.

The tree swallow is perhaps the most common member of this group of perching birds in the North Country. Its preference for a life along forest edges, especially those adjacent to lakes, rivers, marshes, and meadows, makes it well-suited for the environment in this region. Being a cavity nester, the tree swallow can easily be enticed into making its nest in a suitably-sized birdhouse placed on a fencepost, a tree along a lakeshore, or on a pole near a woodland border.

For an insect eater, the tree swallow is an early migrant back to the North Country, beginning to appear during the final days of April. As soon as the ice starts to break up on our lakes, small, widely scattered flocks of these white-bellied birds may be seen cruising over a marsh, pond, or field. While there are never many bugs out during this period of the spring, these hardy swallows seem to be able to find enough to eat to survive until mid-May, when the insect population begins to explode.

The species best known by individuals with a boathouse, barn, or large shed containing an entrance that is left open is the barn swallow. This bird is best recognized by its deeply forked tail, orange underside, and blue back. While it begins arriving in our region during mid-May, it does not start to construct its nest until a little later in the month. Rather than weaving together pieces of straw, the barn swallow collects small mouthfuls of mud which it plasters together to form the framework of its home. The inside is then lined with blades of grass, hairs, feathers, and other similar soft, cushy material.

Its cup-shaped nest is always placed on the upper surface of a beam, wall plate, corner shelf, or other similar structure that affords protection from both the wind and rain. The barn swallow is also known for placing its nest on the bottom plate of a steel I-beam used in bridges. It is not unusual to see a half dozen or more of these dried, earthen nurseries when canoeing under most roads.

In suitable places, there may be several active nests within a few yards of each other, as the barn swallow does not prevent others from nesting nearby. Human presence is also tolerated; however, this bird does get excited when people invade its space and approach its nest too closely. While their tendency to swoop low over your head may be unnerving, and thus, unwelcome, their mud homes should never be disturbed or knocked down. Because they can eat their own weight each day in mosquitoes, black flies, and other insects, especially when they are nesting, swallows are an important control of our insect populations.

A species that is often mistaken for the barn swallow is the cliff swallow. Although similar in appearance, this bird has a light-colored underside and a square-tipped tail. Like the barn swallow, it makes its nest from mouthfuls of mud that are stuck together and then allowed to dry and harden. Rather than construct a cup-shaped nest, the cliff swallow creates a totally enclosed structure that often resembles the shape of a gourd. A cliff swallow may also locate its nest at the top of a vertical wall where a roof can form a ceiling as well as provide protection from the weather. Almost any place that has a surface mud will stick to and will not get wet during a driving rain is likely to be selected by the cliff swallow.

During this time of year, it may seem that our insect population has few natural controls. There are, however, numerous creatures that feast on this bounty of bugs, and the swallows, with their graceful flight, are very near the top of this list.

The Return of the Warblers

No group of birds in the North Country contains such a wide variety of species and is as overall abundant as the warblers. In population studies carried out in stands of maturing forests which are typical of those throughout the Northeast, warblers ranked as the top birds from their arrival during the first weeks of May and continuing until their departure in mid-September.

Yet, despite their prolific numbers, the warblers are not well known. Unlike the robin, blue jay, crow, and chickadee, the many species of warblers that reside in our region do not hop about on the lawn, perch on an exposed limb or telephone line, or frequent a bird feeder. Their preference for a life among the thick foliage of trees and shrubs makes these sparrow-sized birds almost impossible to glimpse, even though some species possess bright-colored plumage at this time of the year. Compounding the problem is the fact that many species of warblers choose to reside in the uppermost sections of trees where they are well hidden from anyone on the ground. The most that is typically seen of these birds is a brief glimpse as they flutter from branch to branch, or dash from a lofty perch to snatch a nearby insect in midair.

Warblers are characterized, in part, by a rather long, delicate bill adapted for grabbing the bugs which comprise their entire diet. After snatching its morsel of animal protein from the air or from the end of a nearby twig, the warbler will quickly return to its perch, which always seems to be hidden behind a clump of leaves or a cluster of needles.

During the middle two weeks of May, the recently-returned warblers are more visible than during any other time of the year. When they arrive from their long migration until the leaves fully erupt from their buds, which is usually just prior to the Memorial Day weekend, visibility into the crowns of deciduous trees and the underbrush that covers the forest floor is still relatively good, although there are still numerous branches and twigs to partially obscure a person's line of sight.

Despite the warblers' stealth-like lifestyle, their presence is made known to passersby during May and June by their frequent, high-pitched calls. Warblers are renowned as songsters, and their melodious calls contribute greatly to the musical richness of our forests, particularly during the early morning and afternoon hours.

While some warblers produce elaborate calls that are difficult to describe, one variety, the ovenbird, bellows out a series of two-note chirps that are easy to recognize. The phrase "tea-cher, tea-cher, tea-cher" is commonly used to

describe this warbler's powerful song. As it rapidly repeats these two notes (the second of which is slightly lower in pitch), the volume seems to increase until it reverberates throughout the forest. Unlike other warblers, the ovenbird prefers a life in the understory, rather than in the canopy. This causes the ovenbird's voice to be occasionally heard coming from some spot close to the forest floor. However, when the males arrive in the area and begin to announce their presence, they often sing well above the ground, which allows their voices to carry a much greater distance.

The black-throated green warbler is another member of this prolific family of woodland birds whose song is easy to identify. This denizen of northern hardwood forests makes a five-note call that is best described by the phrase "Zee-Zee-Zee-Zoo-Zee." All of these notes, given in rapid succession, have the same high pitch except for the next to the last, which is noticeably lower. Like the ovenbird, the black-throated green warbler is exceptionally abundant in heavily wooded settings, and its call is as regular in mature stands of beech, maple, and birch as is the song of the robin in a residential section of a town or village.

During this time of the year and continuing on through the early summer, a wide variety of bird calls can be heard, especially around sunrise and during the early morning hours. While some of these songsters are easy to observe, others are not. Those that defy our attempts to see them are most likely warblers, and as this season progresses, the chances of ever seeing these birds will only diminish.

Lake Trout Move into the Shallows

Sitting atop the food chain in the largest and deepest lakes throughout the North Country is the lake trout, a sizeable, salmon-like creature that, like the other members of this popular group of sport fish, requires cold, well-oxygenated water. Yet, rather than reside in pure mountain rivers or gravel-bottomed streams that are fed by melted snow, this giant, as its name implies, confines its existence to large, deep, crystal-clear northern lakes.

Although all of its relatives prefer a cold environment, the lake trout is especially fond of frigid waters and will seldom stray into places in which the temperature is above fifty degrees. Water that is sixty degrees can be tolerated for only the shortest span of time, and exposure to temperatures that are any higher is lethal to this fish.

As its means of adapting to such cold water, the lake trout has a slightly thicker skin than most of its relatives. Additionally, it develops a higher percentage of body fat in order to better insulate it against the cold. It is not uncommon for a lake trout to have 30 to 40 percent of its body tissue in the form of fat. (One breed of lake trout that occurs in the depths of Lake Superior is reported to be as much as 75 percent fat.) This high concentration of fat gives the lake trout a somewhat oily taste and a flavor not as appealing as that of a brook trout or rainbow trout.

The lake trout's preference for cold water causes it to become most active shortly after the ice goes out during the spring. As the surface water warms to just above 40 degrees, this fish migrates to the shallows where the greatest concentration of food exists. Bays, coves, and stretches of shoreline where the depth of the water is generally less than twenty feet all harbor the small fish and various invertebrates that this aquatic predator consumes.

Because it is normally confined by thermal conditions to the depths of the lake where light intensity is low, the lake trout has evolved eyes that function best in dim light. Consequently, during the spring when it is permitted by cold temperatures to venture near the surface to search for prey, it limits its foraging to those times when the sun has dropped below the horizon or when a heavy overcast exists. Some anglers claim that the best time to fish for lake trout during the spring is on nights when a partial moon is able to illuminate bait a short distance beneath the surface.

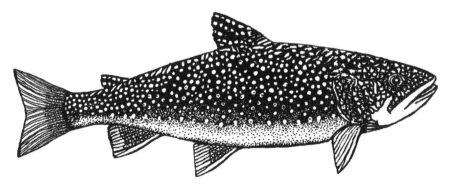

Along with its sense of sight, the lake trout uses its keen sense of smell to locate prey. Chemicals emitted by smaller fish can remain suspended in the water for a fair period of time, and these may be detected by a foraging trout and followed, much like a coyote can track a rabbit, using its nose. While most people are unaware that fish have the ability to detect odors, it is believed by researchers that some species of fish rely as heavily on this sense as any other in gaining information about their surroundings.

Like other fish, a lake trout is also able to detect the presence of other creatures with a band of nerve endings located on its sides. This strip of cells, known as the lateral line, is very sensitive to the vibrations created when an object moves through the water. Some anglers will use lures that wiggle or wobble when slowly dragged, because their vibrations, although tiny, can be sensed by an alert trout. Some fishing experts believe that the noise a person makes in a boat or when slogging into a river with waders can upset or spook a fish that may be feeding nearby. While fish do not have ears like other animals, they certainly have the ability to detect vibrations that propagate through the water, so cautious movement while fishing is always advisable.

As the water continues to warm during the course of May, lake trout gradually retreat into the deeper and colder sections of the lake. Toward the end of June, these leviathans become far more challenging to catch as they move far from the surface. During the spring, however, the shallows are being prowled by some of the largest trout in the northern United States, and hooking one on a fly line or with a lightweight spinning rod can be the fishing experience of a lifetime.

Trillium

At a time when daffodils and tulips are in full bloom in those patches of earth that are cared for by garden enthusiasts, the trillium is beginning to open its petals in places that are tended by no one. And while this woodland wildflower may be encountered in a variety of settings, it is most abundant in mature stands of deciduous trees and mixed hardwood and softwoods, where centuries of decaying leaves, limbs, and bark have created a rich deposit of soil.

85

Trillium is so named because of the arrangement of its major parts in clusters of threes. Its three wide leaves radiate from the top of a stalk that can rise nearly a foot above the forest floor, and its flower is composed of three petals which are separated by three sepals. (Sepals are the green, leaf-like structures that formerly covered the flowering bud.) A detailed analysis of the flower reveals that its ovary is also divided into three chambers and that later, a three-sided berry will form if the flower is successfully pollinated.

In the North Country, three types of trillium are common: the red trillium which supports maroon blossoms, the painted trillium, which bears white petals with muted, dark-red color near its base, and the white trillium, which is colored exactly as its name implies. Botanists also recognize several other species and varieties of these members of the lily family, but the causal hiker or backyard naturalist is likely to note only these three forms.

In many locations, trillium is also known as "stinkpot," as its flowers produce an odor that resembles that of decaying flesh. This is no accident of nature. At this time during the spring, the bodies of those creatures that perished during the winter have thawed and have reached that stage of decay in which the

air surrounding the carcass is noticeably fowled. While this smell is repugnant to humans, it is highly attractive to several forms of insects, such as flies and carrion-feeding beetles that get their nourishment from wildlife corpses. It is these insects the trillium attempts to lure to its flowers to carry out its pollination. The maroon petals of the red trillium, which resemble the color of decaying flesh, further help to reinforce this mimicry of dead matter.

Because flowering, along with the formation of seeds, requires a substantial expenditure of energy, these processes tend to occur in our woodland wildflowers during the brief period in the spring when their exposure to the direct rays of the sun reaches a maximum. This is the time in our deciduous forests when the leaves have not yet completely erupted from their buds. As a result, there is a considerably greater amount of light reaching the forest floor than when the foliage develops and the canopy overhead closes in at the end of May. This is why trillium and most of our other woodland wildflowers are so quick to sprout from their established root system after the snow melts and the upper layer of soil thaws.

Yet while the amount of sunlight reaching the ground is greater than during any other time of the year, there is still adequate shade to keep trillium and its associated wildflowers from becoming overexposed to the sun. Like human skin, the leaves of trillium are sensitive to the harsh ultraviolet rays present in direct sunlight. When placed in the sun for prolonged periods of time, the leaves of trillium eventually become damaged and die. This is why this plant never grows in fields or on the very edge of a patch of woods where sunlight can bake the ground for many hours each day. Also, its root system is not well adapted for functioning during those spells in summer when the ground in open settings becomes parched after a week or two without rain.

Although trillium is one of the most common and highly visible plants in the forests of the Northeast, it should not be picked for display inside a person's home. Unlike those of cultivated flowers, the trillium's blossoms quickly begin to wilt after being severed from its root system. More importantly, its fragrance is not among the most appealing scents, unless you have an attraction to the smell of rotting meat. Consequently, it is best to leave this flower growing undisturbed on the forest floor for passersby to appreciate and bugs to visit.

The Common Toad

The American toad is the only species of toad which exists in the North Country, and it is ordinarily during the middle or end of May when this common amphibian arrives at the shores of various bodies of water to begin its annual breeding activities.

Unlike frogs, the toad is a creature that lives on the forest floor rather than in the water. Anyplace where the air tends to remain relatively cool and humid throughout the day and where there is an ample supply of bugs for it to consume is likely to serve as a home to this familiar critter. Settings in which shade is always present, such as on the north slopes of heavily wooded hillsides or among moss-covered rocks and decaying logs, especially in sheltered ravines, are the places where a toad is most likely to be seen.

Because of its preference for a terrestrial existence, the toad does not retreat during the autumn to the layer of muck that covers the bottom of shallow aquatic settings in order to escape winter's cold. Rather, this slow-hopping animal simply burrows into any soft spot of loose soil on the forest floor. By wiggling and squirming, this somewhat plump amphibian is able to work its way downward through the leaf litter and duff and bury itself below the surface. Even though a toad generally fails to dig itself beneath the frost line, it seldom perishes from the cold because its body is well adapted for surviving temperatures that are below freezing. As a result, while the soil surrounding it may freeze solid, this cold-blooded animal is able to remain alive in a special state of dormancy without having the water in its body turn into ice.

When the soil thaws in spring, the toad awakens and pushes its way upward. Within several days of emerging from its winter retreat, this amphibian instinctively starts to travel toward the body of water from which it came the previous spring. Like frogs, a toad requires water in which to lay its jelly-like eggs. The brush-covered shores of lakes, ponds, and rivers and the weed-laden edges of marshes and alder brooks typically serve as its breeding ground.

Once the male reaches a suitable site, it begins to announce its presence by producing its mating call. The toad emits a pleasant, soft-pitched trilling sound that can last for fifteen to twenty seconds. This sustained, low-intensity trill is most likely to be heard during the evening or at night. A toad is also known to perform its courtship call on days when the air becomes damp or if a female toad should happen to be detected nearby.

The older and larger males are the ones most likely to win the opportunity to mount returning females and fertilize their eggs as they are laid. Unlike frogs, which produce a massive, globular cluster of eggs, toads lay a long, single-file strand. Because of their buoyant nature, these tiny eggs float on the water's surface and are usually attached to one or several objects located near the shore. Upon hatching, the dark-colored embryos emerge as tadpoles. These pollywogs require many weeks of foraging on the microorganisms in these settings before they develop legs and can venture from the aquatic environment.

After laying her eggs, the female leaves the water and returns to the area where she spent the winter. The males tend to remain in the breeding pools for days afterwards, until it appears that no additional females will be arriving at the site.

Despite its slowness, a toad is not often targeted as prey by forest predators. When alarmed, it secretes an incredibly acrid-tasting fluid from glands that exist on its skin. As soon as any creature bites into this amphibian, it is sure to get a mouthful of a chemical that is as bad in taste as that of any naturally occurring

substance. Most predators are believed to attack a toad only once in their lives, as a toad's taste is unpleasant enough to discourage them from even attempting to repeat this specific act of predation.

Although this fluid is exceptionally repulsive in taste, it does not cause any lasting physical impact to a predator, only a psychological one. Additionally, this fluid has no affect on unbroken human skin. Folklore has it that contact with it, such as that which occurs when one picks up a toad, will produce warts. This is not true; however, it is strongly advised that you wash your hands thoroughly after holding a toad, especially if you plan on handling food, because any contact with this substance will provide a horrific taste experience.

The Bittern

There are many sounds that can be heard in and around a marsh during the spring, especially early in the morning and again during the late afternoon and evening. Yet of all the noises and songs that originate from these aquatic, brush-covered areas, the call of the bittern is often deemed the most unusual by those that listen to its natural, seasonal symphony.

The bittern is a fair-sized bird that, though rarely seen, is common throughout the marshes of the North Country. Like its close relative, the great blue heron, the bittern has long legs and toes that are ideally adapted for standing in shallow water and wading through places where the bottom is covered with dead aquatic grasses, weeds, and muck.

Unlike its heron cousin, the bittern shies away from open water where it can be clearly seen. Rather, it confines all of its activities to places where small shrubs and other dwarf woody plants cluster together to form a dense thicket several feet above the water's surface. The streaked gray, tan, and brown plumage that the bittern supports causes this recluse of northern marshes to perfectly match the surrounding plants. So effective is its camouflage that when the bittern senses danger, it responds by immediately placing its long and narrow bill straight upward and puffing out its neck feathers, rather than taking to the air. A researcher once observed a bittern swaying back and forth in unison with the plants around it as they were being moved by the wind, as if in a deliberate attempt to blend in with the background and avoid being detected.

Since its protective coloration is so effective, the female bittern tends to remain on her nest whenever an intruder happens to come into the immediate area, rather than attempt to draw its attention away from the scene as many birds do. Some wildlife photographers and researchers have been able to approach a hen

within a foot or two as she sits on her nest without causing her to flush. Because of this tendency to remain perfectly still and not take to the air, the bittern is most often overlooked by those who walk or canoe past the wading bird that some people have nicknamed the "mud hen."

While the bittern is not easy to spot, the call produced by the male is unmistakable and can resonate up to a half mile or more across the weed- and shrub-covered aquatic terrain. During the spring, the bittern maintains control of a given section of marsh by producing a bizarre, three-note call that has been described as resembling the sound produced by an old, wooden-handled well pump.

The phrase "glum-pa-dunk" is used to represent this call. Although the first and third notes are longer than the second, the middle note seems to be emphasized more both in intensity and pitch. At the beginning of its song, the bittern gulps down as much air as possible into its crop (a throat pouch normally used to hold food). It then forces the air back up into its mouth and down again, which results in this unusual avian sound. Ordinarily the male will repeat this three-note phrase from three to seven times in sequence before emptying its throat of air.

Because life thrives in water, wetlands of all types are able to support a greater diversity of life than any other ecological setting. Throughout May and into June in the North Country, the array of mating songs from both amphibians and birds is unequaled. While the odds that you will ever see a bittern meander its way through the marsh vegetation or maintaining its statue-like pose are not great, the chances of eventually hearing the weird "glum-pa-dunk" call of this bird echo from the small shrubs, dried cattails, and newly-sprouting rushes that cover these sites are fairly good. It is a call unlike any other bird's and most definitely worth hearing.

The Red-Backed Salamander

Living hidden among the dead leaves and decaying needles that cover the forest floor is the red-backed salamander, a small amphibian believed by many naturalists to be the most common form of vertebrate life in the woodlands throughout the Northeast. With densities reported as high as one to two individuals per square yard, no other higher form of life matches it in overall numbers. Additionally, some biologists maintain that the red-backed salamander is also, pound for pound, at the very top of the list of vertebrates in nearly all forested settings.

Yet despite its abundance, the red-backed salamander is not among our most conspicuous or visible forms of life. Like other amphibians, this secretive creature is extremely sensitive to dry conditions, causing it to be active only at night once the air has become saturated with moisture. Its dark color, small size, silent nature, and preference for foraging in the layer of dead organic matter on the forest floor prevents it from drawing any attention to itself.

As daylight approaches, this salamander returns to a favored spot, such as a large chunk of fallen bark, a rotted log, or a rock, and wriggles its way beneath it. In such a tight enclosure, it can better retain the moisture essential for its skin, as well as avoid being seen by the all-too-numerous predators that enjoy dining on its small, yet meaty carcass.

Should a red-backed salamander be uncovered by some natural enemy, it immediately turns its back and attempts to crawl away and become hidden in the leaf litter. Since its tail is covered with a most unpleasant tasting secretion, the first mouthful that a predator normally gets causes it to instantly discontinue its attack. Also, like some lizards, the red-backed salamander can shed its tail in order to escape the clutches of an enemy. Once detached, the tail will wiggle and twitch involuntarily for a short period of time in a further attempt to distract an attacker from the place

into which the salamander has retreated.

Regenerating this lost tissue, as well as replacing the fat stored in this appendage, places a salamander under a fair amount of nutritional stress. A female that loses a tail will often forego laying eggs that year in order to channel her energy into the growth of a new one.

Unlike the many amphibians whose choruses are heard in various watery settings at this time of the year, the red-backed salamander produces no mating call and does not seek out an aquatic setting in which to mate and lay its eggs. After emerging from its winter dormancy in the soil, a male begins his annual search for females using his exceptionally keen sense of smell. Once a potential mate is located, it is believed by naturalists that he advertises his worth as a breeding partner by providing some of his excrement for her analysis. An individual that controls an area rich in the ground invertebrates upon which this salamander feeds will have feces that reflects his success and superior standing compared to others that have not been as fortunate.

Some weeks after breeding, the female will lay her jelly-like cluster of eggs in a damp, sheltered spot on the forest floor. Like its daytime retreat, an egg-laying site is a place of great worth to this salamander, and it is defended against intrusion by any and all individuals. The eggs may take another month or more to hatch, and the female will guard them during that time to keep them from being eaten by other foraging animals. During dry periods, she will wrap her long body around the cluster in an attempt to prevent them from dehydrating, while during unusually wet weather, she will rub the egg mass with her tail in order to coat its surface with a secretion that prevents the growth of mold and bacteria.

By late spring, the eggs will hatch, yielding tiny individuals that quickly develop the physical likeness and behavior patterns of an adult. This is in sharp contrast to other amphibians that first experience a tadpole stage in which their appearance and habits are markedly different than those of their parents.

Beneath the many objects on the forest floor there lives a rich array of animals that are seldom noticed, even by experienced naturalists. In this habitat of rotting leaves, dead twigs, and decomposing chunks of bark and wood, the red-backed salamander is the most abundant vertebrate, and it is during this time in the spring that it is attempting to add to its already high numbers.

Bullheading

During the latter part of the spring, particularly on pleasant nights, people may be seen sitting in lawn chairs near a lantern placed directly on the shore of a pond, marsh, or lake where the water is shallow and mucky. While relaxation and social camaraderie are the primary reasons many are lured there, the hopes of catching a mess of bullhead is also at the forefront of most such gatherings. Although this tasty member of the catfish family may be caught at any time of the day during the warmer months of the year, late evening during early June is the period when the bullhead is most active and likely to bite on a baited hook.

Because a bullhead functions best in warm waters, this fish tends to concentrate its time in shallow areas that have a dark bottom or which contain a high concentration of suspended organic debris, settings that are the most effective in converting the sun's rays into heat. Waterways that are clear and sparkling reflect a high percentage of sunlight and are less capable of absorbing the thermal energy of the sun.

Like most fish, a bullhead's preferred diet consists almost entirely of bugs, but snails, small crayfish, worms, insect larvae, nymphs of all sorts and sizes, and other types of aquatic invertebrates are also sought out for consumption. Because the murky underwater conditions severely limit visibility, the bullhead has evolved the ability to locate a morsel of animal matter by its well-developed senses of touch and taste. The eight whisker-like appendages which surround its mouth, known as barbells, are its primary sensory organs. Using them to gently probe the upper layer of muck, a bullhead is able to identify items to eat by their feel and flavor.

Once it's located, the bullhead pulls a potential meal into its mouth by a siphoning action. This process of sucking up a bug or two also causes algae and

other forms of plankton that abound on the bottom to be pulled into the bull-head's exceptionally wide mouth – and the well-adapted creature swallows it all. Over the course of its evolutionary history, the bullhead has developed the ability to derive nourishment from both the plants and animals that occur in the surface muck. This infusion of vegetable matter into a bullhead's diet allows this fish to be more omnivorous than any other fish that exists in the North Country.

Because bullheads do not rely on eyesight to locate food, this fish has developed nocturnal feeding habits. Such nightly foraging tactics greatly reduce its risk of being preyed upon by the many carnivores that enjoy dining on such a meaty fish. A life in relatively shallow water subjects an aquatic creature to the threat of attack from the air above, and the osprey and bald eagle are two of a handful of birds that will attempt to catch a fish that comes too close to the surface. By prowling for food under the cover of darkness, the bullhead not only eliminates the chances of being snagged by one of these diurnal birds of prey, but also reduces the likelihood of being spotted by an otter, mink, or the great blue heron which is known to hunt the shallows after sunset.

The bullhead additionally discourages attack by possessing an exceedingly sharp spine on the leading edge of its dorsal and pectoral fins. When threatened, it holds these needle-like bones directly outward, so that an enemy is likely to suffer a painful puncture wound when the bullhead is grabbed. A person should always exercise the utmost caution when handling a bullhead, as this method of defense may also pose a danger to a human's hand. Some people always take hold of a bullhead by the lower lip as there are no sharp spines around its mouth. Other anglers grab this fish by the face with their fingers held well clear of its front fins.

Unlike other North Country fish, the bullhead possesses a smooth and completely scaleless skin which is capable of absorbing small amounts of oxygen into its body. A bullhead is also able to take in oxygen by gulping air at the surface. These two alternate methods of acquiring this life-sustaining gas are essential to a fish that spends much of its time in waters that are critically low in oxygen concentration.

As a means of improving the chance that its eggs and recently hatched young will survive, the bullhead employs a strategy that is normally associated with more advanced forms of life. After spawning, which typically occurs toward the end of June in the North Country, the adult will remain around the nest in order to chase away any creature that strays too near. After the eggs hatch, both parents guard their offspring for several weeks until their swimming skills develop and they are able to quickly scramble under cover when danger arises.

Yet another aspect of the bullhead that sets it apart from other fish is the taste of its flesh. It is this feature that lures anglers to the edges of marshes, ponds, and shallow lakes after the sun sets during this time of the year.

June Bugs

Coinciding with the first outbreak of true summer weather, a time when windows can be left open throughout the night, is the emergence of the adult June beetle, known to some as the June bug. This large, chestnut-colored beetle makes its presence known after dusk, as it repeatedly crashes into screens, especially those that have a lamp close by. The June bug may also be heard slamming into the side of a house near a porch light, or noisily buzzing against a pane of glass through which a light is shinning. Occasionally, one or several dead specimens may be found in the morning beneath the window or door into which they had forcefully flown.

The June bug is one of the larger beetles which occurs in the North Country, as it can grow to be nearly an inch in length. Like other beetles, it possesses a front set of "wings" that fold perfectly over its back to form an armor-like shell. The rear wings, which are used for flight, are considerably larger and nearly transparent. Since they fold neatly beneath the front set when the beetle comes to rest, these wings are only seen when the beetle is buzzing against a window or screen.

Nearly all of the June bugs that appear in the darkness during a warm June night are males that are traveling about in an attempt to locate a breeding partner. The females, which seldom take to the air, are known to emit a special odor when the time comes for their eggs to be fertilized. Upon detecting this scent, the male will immediately home in on the precise location of the source and join the female there.

After mating, the female lays her eggs in the soil, and within a month they have hatched into small, white, worm-like entities known as grubs. At first, the larvae feast on pieces of organic matter in the soil. As they grow and their mouth develops, the grubs begin to spend an increasing amount of time gnawing on the tiniest pieces of tissue projecting from the roots of plants.

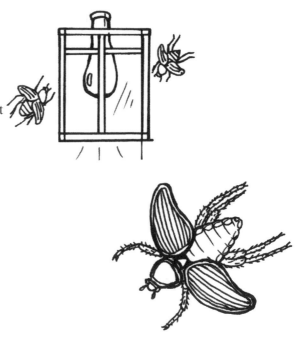

When the soil cools during mid-autumn, the grubs cease feeding and work their way down into the dirt. To keep from freezing to death, they burrow several feet below the surface before entering a period of dormancy that lasts until the spring. With the thawing of the soil, the grubs migrate upward to an area in which roots exist in a concentrated form. During this second summer, they develop a ravenous appetite and have been known to wreak havoc on the roots of grasses, garden vegetables, and various types of cultivated flowers. Occasionally, an infestation of grubs may consume enough of a lawn's root system that large sections of the turf can be readily pealed from the soil.

The fairly large size and meaty texture of this grub makes it a prize for numerous insect-eating creatures. The skunk has an uncanny ability to sense grubs just below the surface and will excavate small holes in an attempt to harvest these larvae. These holes in a person's lawn, particularly toward the end of summer, are an indication that this grub predator has been at work in the area. Numerous species of birds, including the crow, are also adept at locating and extracting these pests from a lawn. Moles are yet another natural enemy of the June bug larvae and can be quite effective in containing a grub infestation.

The grubs that are successful in surviving until autumn repeat the process of the previous year, migrating underground before the surface freezes and reemerging in the spring to that section of the ground which is rich in roots. At the onset of summer, the two-year-old larva begins the period of pupation that eventually ends with its transformation into an adult June bug. Yet, rather than emerge into the air, the adult retains its subterranean existence and eventually burrows well down into the dirt a third time to pass another winter.

After the soil has completely thawed and warmed, the adult will finally pull itself above ground for the first time. The adult June bug feeds mainly on the leaves of deciduous trees, especially those of maples. Feeding always occurs at night; each day, with the approach of dawn, the June bug will retreat just below the surface of the soil.

Naturalists are still unsure why this nocturnal beetle hurls itself towards the artificial light coming from a house, persistently banging against whatever stands in its way. While screens are designed to keep out mosquitoes and other noxious biting flies, the wire mesh is also an effective barrier to this bug. Meanwhile, the noise the June bug makes while buzzing against this metallic fabric or hitting a pane of glass is a well known part of life during June in the North Country.

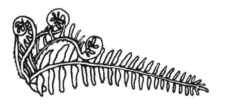

The Kingfisher

Periodically occurring around ponds, marshes, shallow bays on lakes, and stretches of rivers that support healthy populations of small, four- to five-inch fish is a medium-sized blue-colored bird known as the belted kingfisher. With its distinct rattling-chatter call and the unique, "electrified" profile created by a jagged row of feathers on the top and back of its head, the kingfisher is not easy to mistake for any other bird associated with the water.

Upon its return in mid-spring after the ice has completely melted from our waterways, the kingfisher is quick to establish a feeding territory around a suitable aquatic setting. When searching for a meal, this bird will either perch on a limb that overhangs the water by ten to fifteen feet, or it will hover in midair by beating its wings in a rapid manner. Once it spots a small fish, the kingfisher dives head first into the water in an attempt to grab its prey with its pointed bill.

Along with laying claim to a favorable stretch of shoreline, the kingfisher must also establish a nesting territory. Unlike every other species of bird in the North Country, with the exception of the bank swallow, the kingfisher seeks out a steep cliff into which it will excavate a burrow, preferring a slope that is more than ten feet in height, composed of sand or other soft soil, and containing little if any vegetation. A hillside composed of hard-packed gravel is generally ignored, as the kingfisher is not adequately adapted for tunneling into stone-laden material. A slope that is not exceedingly steep is likewise rejected, as such a site

would fail to keep intruders from gaining access to the entrance. While a cliff that is within shouting distance from the water is most favorable, the kingfisher has been known to travel as far as a mile inland to a nesting site that meets its requirements if one closer to the water cannot be found.

It is the male that searches the area for a nesting site, and he is the one that eventually lays claim to the earthen face that will contain the family nest. In order to work in dirt that lacks topsoil and avoid tree roots, the kingfisher usually locates the entrance to its nest at least two feet below the crest of the cliff. This also is far enough down the face of the bank to prevent a predator from stumbling upon the opening.

After the male pairs up with a female, both birds begin the process of excavating a hole in the side of the embankment. The kingfisher loosens the soil with its pointed bill, much as a woodpecker dislodges chunks of dead bark from a tree trunk. As the soil falls, it is forcefully kicked backwards. Initially the dirt can be flung out the entrance with little difficulty; however, as the passageway lengthens, it begins to take an increasingly greater amount of effort to remove the loosened earth from the tunnel. It has been noted by researchers that a pair of kingfishers can dig horizontally almost a foot into the bank on their first day of work. However, progress further inward slows as more time must be spent kicking the soil out of the hole.

After completing roughly three feet of tunnel, the birds dig an oval-shaped chamber that serves as the nesting site. Ordinarily, a half-dozen white eggs are deposited on the floor of this chamber and then incubated by both parents over the course of the next three and a-half weeks. After hatching, the young birds will remain within the earthen cavity for roughly one month, while both parents continually travel to their feeding territory to obtain small fish for them to eat. The warming of the water following Memorial Day causes many small fish to venture near the surface and come within striking distance of the kingfisher. This makes it possible for the adults to catch the fish needed to sustain the rapidly developing nestlings. The abundance of small fish near the surface later during the summer also helps to increase the likelihood that the fledglings will catch fish when they begin to dive for their own meals.

Because of the widespread availability of favorable freshwater habitat, the kingfisher is quite common throughout the North Country. With a little patience, it is possible for an onlooker to see a kingfisher plunge into the water and emerge with a fish in its bill, particularly at this time of year. By observing the direction in which a bird with a fish in its mouth is flying, it may also be possible, with a little luck, to locate the sandy slope in which this unique bird is rearing the next generation of kingfishers.

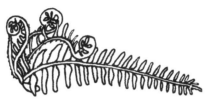

Osprey Nesting Time

Although there are many forms of wildlife that feed on fish throughout the North Country, the osprey is at the very top of the area's aquatic food chain. With a body that can be in excess of three pounds and wings that may span five feet from tip to tip, this diurnal raptor is without a definite natural enemy other than man. Its size and strength allow it to prey on the larger fish that inhabit our waters. Ordinarily, six- to twelve-inch fish are the osprey's target, yet it is known to periodically take individuals that are up to sixteen inches in length and three pounds in weight. As a result, the osprey is the only raptor in the North Country that can haul an animal which nears its own body weight through the air.

Diving from a height of up to forty feet, this massive bird can plunge below the surface when going after a meal. The osprey's long legs extend its reach so that it may successfully latch onto a fish that is over a foot from the surface. The sharp-pointed talons of this predator easily slice into the scaly covering of its quarry, and their long, hook shape is adapted to deeply penetrate into the fish and secure it in the osprey's grasp. Small prongs on the bottom of its feet also help to prevent a slippery catch from wiggling free.

The return of the osprey to the North Country in the spring coincides with the disappearance of ice from the larger bodies of water. During this period, the osprey is often able to snag trout that rise to the surface to feast on the insects that congregate there, and its keen eyesight allows it to detect the disturbances on the surface caused by a fish that is cruising below. As the water warms during the spring and trout begin to migrate into deeper waters, bullhead, suckers, and perch become the staple in the osprey's diet.

An osprey seen soaring over a lake, pond or river may initially be mistaken for a large gull because of their similar white undersides. Also, the osprey's aerial profile, which is characterized by a distinct bend near the middle of the wing, superficially resembles the way a gull holds its wings when it is riding air currents. Differences include the shape of an osprey's head, its overall larger size,

and subtle color differences – all of which can be used to distinguish between this raptor and our region's common avian scavenger.

Shortly after returning to the North Country, the osprey, like most other birds, begins the process of nesting. Older individuals instinctively go back to the structure that served as their nest during previous years. These tend to be located atop a tall tree that has an unobstructed view of the entire surroundings. Occasionally, the osprey will utilize a platform set on top of a utility pole by electric companies, who erect them in cooperation with conservation organizations in locations where transmission lines run through settings that are favorable to the bird.

The stick nest constructed by the osprey averages four feet in diameter and two feet in height. Each year the pair of birds adds to its massive collection of twigs until the nest may reach eight feet across and measure over four feet in depth. While both adults collect sticks, it is the male that gathers the bulk of these twigs. The female concentrates more on weaving them into a sturdy configuration and obtaining the soft, cushiony matter that lines the inside.

During mid-spring, two to three eggs are laid over the course of a three- to five-day period of time. The female does most of the incubation, which lasts for five to five and a-half weeks. (The exact number of days needed for the eggs to hatch is believed to depend on the relative warmth of the season.) Like other large birds of prey, osprey nestlings are slow to develop; it takes three weeks before they start to exercise their wings, and it is not for a month or more that the young birds leave their nest for their first short flight.

Beginning with incubation and continuing until the birds fledge, the female osprey only occasionally leaves the nest to search for fish. Most of her food during this period is brought to her by her mate. Throughout June and July, the time when the nestlings are clamoring for fish, the male does little else than hunt for food.

Even though both adults support nearly identical plumage, it is possible to distinguish between the sexes at this time of year by watching them for a short while, as the birds engage in completely different activities in late spring and early summer. Should you happen to spot an osprey flying overhead during this month or the next with a fish in its talons, it is safe to assume that the individual is a male. For the next two months, it will be the female who sits mainly on the nest, which tends to be clearly visible from the surroundings below.

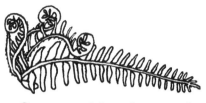

Orange Hawkweed

Among the numerous forms of vegetation that grow throughout the North Country is orange hawkweed, the plant that is responsible for producing the attractive orange cast to many sun-filled sites during the latter part of June. Like its distant relative the dandelion, orange hawkweed is considered by naturalists to be one of the region's most easily recognized and abundant "wildflowers." But to the many homeowners with scattered patches of it covering their lawns, or to the farmer that must prevent it from taking over valuable pastures, this plant, also known as devil's paintbrush, is considered to be one of the region's most notorious "weeds."

Like many plants that thrive in open areas, orange hawkweed is of European origin and not native to this continent. It is believed to have been brought to North America during the early 1800s for use in gardens because of its hardy nature and colorful flowering head. Since its seeds are easily dispersed by the wind, it was not too long before the plant began appearing in increasingly scattered locations, and by the end of the nineteenth century it had eventually spread throughout much of the East.

Once a single plant takes hold, it can quickly multiply at that spot, as orange hawkweed also reproduces by means of runners or rhizoids, the lengthy lateral shoots just below its circular cluster of leaves. These vine-like structures grow out to nearly a foot before sprouting a new plant. In this manner, a single orange hawkweed can give rise to a fairly dense patch of plants within a decade.

Like most weeds, the devil's paintbrush is able to flourish in places where the soil is only fair to marginal. In the North Country, the strip of land adjacent to roads develops a sandy texture, and repeated exposure to road salt further diminishes the soil quality, yet the plant grows even there. Aside from the sides of highways, orange hawkweed grows well in the treeless swaths beneath electrical transmission lines, particularly in places where the bedrock lies close to the surface, or where sand or gravel are present, conditions which limit numerous other plants from developing there. Richer soil can support plants that are able to out-compete this hawkweed species for growing space.

Unfortunately, lawns that occur in places where the soil is less than fertile also frequently harbor orange hawkweed, much to the dismay of homeowners who wish to see only grass. Since its leaves form a basal rosette or a dense circular plane that lies flat on the ground, the plant is rarely damaged by mowing. While a mower may sever its tall, hair-covered flowering stalk, cutting the lawn lowers the height of the grass that grows around the plant, increasing the amount of sunlight received by its leaves and actually helping it grow. And attempts to eradicate orange hawkweed by pulling it up after it becomes established are an exercise in futility. Inevitably, one or several runners break off from the uprooted plant and allow for continued regeneration at that spot.

While wildflowers, such as the daisy, clover, Queen Anne's lace, and goldenrod blossom for weeks on end, orange hawkweed's reign of predominance is fairly short lived. By the end of June, most of its characteristic orange flow-

ers have transformed into small, fuzzy clusters of seeds. Scattered plants may continue to bloom through July, especially in places where shade is present for a portion of the day, but they will fail to produce massive patches.

Unlike many wildflowers, orange hawkweed cannot be picked for display indoors. Within minutes after being detached from the plant, the flowers close and the stalk withers, even if immediately placed in water. The only way to enjoy the beauty of orange hawkweed is to admire it as it grows wild, provided that you are one of the few who sees this plant as a treasure of nature, rather than as the repulsive weed most people consider it to be.

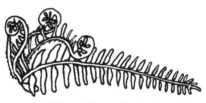

The Cowbird

In general appearance and basic mating behavior, the brown-headed cowbird is not much different from any other bird, but when it comes to nesting, this feathered creature is quite unlike any other species of bird in all of North America. Rather than spend time and expend energy constructing a nest, incubating eggs, tending to the needs of the nestlings, and caring for the young immediately after they have learned to fly, the cowbird simply deposits its eggs in the nest of another bird and entrusts the occupants to become good foster parents.

After returning from their wintering ranges in the southern United States, cowbirds pair up for their breeding season, which begins in mid-May. The female selects and establishes a territory, usually in a fair-sized stand of hardwood trees. The male that has claimed the corresponding area then becomes her mate for the approximately two-month breeding period.

Deciduous woodland edges are sought out by the cowbird as these sites typically harbor the greatest concentration of nesting songbirds. The availability of food does not seem to be of any concern to the cowbird when it selects a breeding territory, because it typically searches for food elsewhere. Semi-brushy areas, meadows, and pasturelands are all favored feeding sites. Places ideal for grazing dairy cattle are especially attractive, hence this bird's name, and it is common to see it in small flocks in cow pastures throughout the afternoon, even during June.

Each morning after it has been fertilized, the female will quietly watch and follow the movements of any robins, thrushes, vireos, warblers, or other similarly-sized birds within her breeding territory. Once she pinpoints the location of a nest, the cowbird will hide nearby until both parents leave. As soon as the nest is unattended, the cowbird quickly enters and lays one of its own eggs in that nest. If it is able to, this social parasite will push one of the resident eggs out (should there be any eggs already laid in the nest) in an attempt to trick the host into believing that nothing has changed during its brief absence.

Periods of cold, inclement weather can seriously impact the ability of a cowbird to successfully invade a nest. When the temperature is unseasonably chilly, or when a steady rain is falling, brooding birds are extremely reluctant to leave their eggs, even for the shortest period of time. Also, during times of nasty weather, the male tends to quickly replace his mate when it becomes necessary for her to leave the nest.

As is the case with nearly all birds, the female cowbird lays her eggs in the morning. After successfully depositing an egg, she quickly exits the area and frequently begins her effort to locate another potential host for the next day. Since

the chance of any bird rearing two orphans is nil, the cowbird never returns to the same nest. Because one female cowbird excludes all other females from entering her territory, it is highly unlikely that another cowbird will lay an egg in a nest the resident female has already victimized.

The cowbird will continue to search for new nests throughout June and occasionally into early July. Over the course of the breeding season, a single cowbird may lay in excess of three dozen eggs.

As a rule, the reaction of most birds to the presence of a foreign egg in their nest is not favorable. Some have been observed pushing the unwanted egg out of the nest, while others abandon that nest and start a new one. Some birds will tolerate the additional egg, but once it hatches, the cowbird nestling is either neglected or pushed from the nest. Inevitably, however, there are always a few pairs of birds in the territory of a cowbird that will incubate the eggs and care for the nestling until it can fend for itself.

Despite its upbringing by individuals of a different species, a young cowbird does not develop any of the habits of its foster parents, nor does it form any ties to them. As soon as it has grown to the stage at which it becomes independent, the young bird instinctively seeks out other cowbirds. Eventually larger flocks form, and the next year, these individuals will repeat this unique style of reproduction.

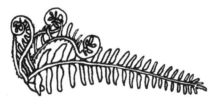

Firefly Season

The aurora borealis, lightning, and meteor showers are all premier light shows of nature that are sometimes spectacular and on other occasions contain only very subtle beauty. During the first few weeks of summer in the North Country, another of nature's nocturnal displays of light may be seen in and around open and overgrown fields and brushy forest clearings when fireflies enter into their breeding season.

As is the case with other creatures, fireflies advertise their presence to members of the opposite sex when the time for mating arrives. Rather than rely on some form of vocalization or the release of pheromones, the chemicals used by animals to communicate via their sense of smell, fireflies produce pulses of light to attract attention.

Repeatedly flying over areas in which females reside, the male advertises his availability to breed by displaying an appropriate sequence of flashes, hoping to catch the eye of a member of the opposite sex that has reached a similar stage in her life cycle. When a female spots his luminescent call, she will respond with a flash that lets her suitor know she is receptive to his advances. The female is seldom forced to take to the air in search of a mate, because her call tends to be immediately answered by any and all males in the area.

After mating, the male will continue to prowl the air space over his chosen territory in an attempt to repeat this reproductive act. Nearly all of the flashes that are visible as the summer twilight fades over fields and brushy shorelines are those of the males.

Since a number of different species of fireflies can occupy the same general habitat, each has evolved its own particular light code that will identify it to its own kind. The duration of the flash and the time between pulses are the main characteristics that distinguish one species from another. Their aerial movements – whether they are ascending, looping, traveling in a horizontal line, or hovering while signaling – are also different for each species and aid in firefly recognition. Additionally, not all fireflies emit the exact same color of light – some produce a more yellowish glow, while others have a slightly greenish tint to their beacon.

Consequently, a person with an eye for detail may be able to differentiate among the various flashes and identify the active species.

Like any highly visible courtship ritual, that of the male firefly may draw the attention of a natural enemy rather than a potential mate. While there are several creatures that will prey on airborne fireflies, one of the most menacing threats confronting these luminescent beetles is from a certain larger species of fireflies. When they detect the flashing pattern given by the male of a smaller species, some bigger, more predatory fireflies will mimic the response elicited by the female of that smaller species. As soon as the expectant male lands next to it, the larger firefly will attack and attempt to kill it. Some researchers have reported that there are predatory fireflies that can very effectively mimic the light signal of three or four separate species.

These scientists have also observed that the males of such larger species are occasionally drawn toward the light flashes produced by the females of smaller species. In such instances, they believe the male hopes to find a mimicking female of his own species that he may be able to entice into breeding.

Unquestionably, the tiny flickers produced by these beetles do not compare in power to the display that is evident during Fourth of July celebrations. However, to the naturalist whose goal it is to observe, analyze, and decipher them, these minute twinkles can be every bit as entertaining.

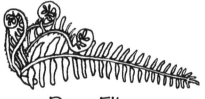

Deer Flies

The start of the summer in the North Country can be marked by many events, and among the least desirable is the resurgence of the population of deer flies. While the black fly makes a nuisance of itself during the late spring by swarming around a person's head in large numbers, no black fly is able to inflict as much pain when it bites, or to continually persist to pierce a person's skin after being repeatedly swatted as the deer fly can.

Like other biting flies, the deer fly spends its larval stage in the water.

Marshes, bogs, the shores of lakes and ponds, and the quiet backwater of rivers are the types of aquatic settings most preferred by this bug during its immature stage. In such shallow places, the worm-like maggot often partially buries itself in the soft muck. Some entomologists have reported that deer fly larva feed entirely on the abundance of rotting plant matter that exists there. However, other researchers believe that deer fly larva may act like their very close relatives, the horse fly, and prey on the rich variety of small invertebrates that also occur in quiet, fresh water environments.

As it readies to metamorphosize into an adult during early to mid-June, the larva must move from the water to a dry location. Because the pupa gets oxygen from the air rather than the water, the larva must situate itself in a dry spot as it nears this next phase of its life cycle. During most years in our region, water levels naturally drop with the approach of summer, as drier weather couples with the final exhaustion of the snow pack in the mountains. As a result, the deer fly larva is not forced to move much, if at all, when it comes time for it to enter into its dormant pupa stage.

During years when frequent and prolonged rainstorms lead to a sudden and substantial rise of the water level, deer fly pupa may drown in the flooding. In some areas, localized deer fly populations can be intentionally reduced by temporarily elevating the water level during this pupation period.

After emerging into the adult stage, both males and females feed on the nectar of various flowers. Males, which are incapable of biting, can be identified by the extremely large size of their eyes, which are said to be large enough that they can touch each other and seem to cover a majority of the insect's head.

During the evening, the males congregate toward the very top of the tallest trees, where they wait for the females to find them. After breeding, the females travel to the forest edges and woodland clearings where deer most often reside. Like other biting flies, the female deer fly needs a meal of blood in order for the eggs developing inside of her to properly form, and the whitetail is the favorite target for obtaining this protein-enriched fluid. Moose, horses, cows, and other large animals – including humans – are also routinely attacked.

Like the horsefly, the deer fly relies primarily on its keen sense of sight to locate a host, with movement and color believed to be the features that catch the attention of a pregnant female. When it detects a potential victim, the deer fly will rapidly fly in a circle around its target in an attempt to assess the safest place to land. This is usually in a spot where it can burrow into the fur of its host, so as not to be knocked off when swatted by a tail or shaken loose when the creature violently twitches its muscles. A deer fly also has an especially hard exoskeleton that provides it with a fair degree of protection, even when it's severely swatted. All too often a deer fly will drop to the ground after being hit by a person's hand, only to recover from the blow and initiate another attack.

Shortly after landing, the deer fly inserts a saw-like mouth piece into the creature's skin and begins to cut deep enough to sever surface capillaries. As drops of blood form on the wound, the deer fly laps it up with its sponge-like tongue.

Within a day or two of absorbing its meal of blood, the female returns to a place with shallow water. As a rule, she places her cluster of eggs, which can number up to a hundred, on the leaf of a plant that overhangs the water. Upon hatching, the larvae fall into the water and begin the cycle again.

Because the deer fly requires a fair amount of light to find a host, its period of activity is limited to the daytime, especially while the sun is out. This is why any individual deer fly that becomes trapped inside is immediately drawn toward a window or the glass in a door. Consequently, if you wish to avoid an encounter with the deer fly, it is best to limit your outdoor activities to the very early morning, late afternoon, or periods of heavy overcast or rain. But when a deer fly does happen to attack, it is best to simply let it land and give it a few seconds to secure a spot on your skin. It is then possible to crush it between your thumb and index finger, as swatting is an all too ineffective method of killing this resilient pest of the early summer.

July

The Green Frog and Bullfrog

If you're standing near or walking along a marshy shoreline during July, it is likely you will hear the sound of a frog. As the water begins to warm to a temperature that is tolerable for swimming, aquatic frogs start to spend an increasing amount of time on the process of mating. As is the case with all tailless amphibians, it is the male that is responsible for producing the vocalization that alerts females in the immediate vicinity of his willingness to fertilize eggs.

In the North Country, there are a half dozen species of frogs, and of these, the green frog and bullfrog are the most common and the ones most likely to be heard. As is the case with songbirds, it is easier to note the presence of a frog during its breeding season through sound, which carries a fair distance, rather than by sight.

Each species has its own distinct call, and their periodic vocalizations announce that they are in residence. The sound of the green frog is most likely to be heard in waterways that are shallow and contain weedy sections of shoreline. From early June through the end of July, this greenish-brown amphibian, which averages three to four inches in length, bellows out its single-note call. Sounding very much like a plucked string on a cello or bass viol, this brief note can be heard sporadically throughout the day and especially during the evening. It is generated as air from the frog's overly inflated lungs is forced into two vocal sacs located on the lower sides of its throat. As the air rushes over its vocal cords, these larynx structures vibrate, thereby creating the green frog's characteristic song. Once these pouches are filled, the air can then be pushed back towards the lungs again, which allows the animal to repeat its resonant call.

The bullfrog, along with several other related amphibians, has only a single vocal pouch situated on the underside of its throat. Should you happen to spot one of these large frogs in the act of singing, you'll see that its large size appears to be expanded by the greatly swollen nature of its throat. The presence of a bullfrog can be quickly verified by the low-pitched, slow-paced "jug-o-rum" call it emits. Ordinarily, this four- to six-inch-long, green-colored amphibian resides in sizeable aquatic settings, such as along the weedy shores of lakes; however, the bullfrog can also be heard around the edges of some larger ponds and in the backwaters of slowly flowing rivers.

As is the situation with most forms of wildlife, the bullfrog's vocalization can put it in danger because it alerts predators that a meal is nearby. Naturalists have discovered that the snapping turtle is keyed into the auditory love notes of these amphibians and will react accordingly when one is within shouting distance. This is why a singing frog may seem more wary than one that is simply sunning itself on the shore.

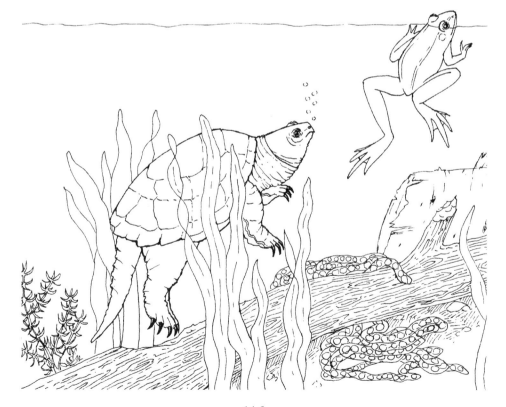

The wood frog, spring peeper, and toad all favor relatively dry sites to hunt for invertebrate matter. Yet in order to breed in the spring, these amphibians must return to the water, congregating at the nearest pond, marsh, or drainage ditch that has conditions that are favorable for their eggs and resulting tadpoles. These synchronized, short-distance migrations result in a relatively large number of breeding adults simultaneously gathering at the same general location. This is why there are often impressive choruses of peeping, trilling, and clacking sounds during evenings in the spring.

Because both the green frog and bullfrog are instinctively inclined to reap the bounty of bugs that exist in and just over the surface of the water, neither is forced to leave its feeding ranges when overcome by the urge to breed. As a result, their calls are usually heard coming from varied waterside locations, and they also tend to be quite sporadic, as opposed to the songs of their terrestrial counterparts, which sound more steady and in harmony.

As the summer progresses, the sound of singing green frogs and bullfrogs gradually declines. This leaves only the increasing chorus of crickets, and of course, the irritating hum of the mosquito, as the accompaniment for an evening outing along the shores of a mountain pond or marsh.

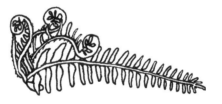

Dealing with Summer's Heat

Although the members of our wildlife community are better adapted for dealing with winter's cold, all of the creatures that inhabit the North Country during the summer are capable of coping with those few situations when the mercury nears the 90 degree mark.

During bouts of unseasonably hot weather, diurnal animals tend to concentrate their activities to the times of the day when the air temperature is relatively cool. Creatures like the red squirrel and chipmunk are known to shift their midday routines to the early morning and late afternoon and evening hours, times when the sun is not as hot and the temperature is less oppressive.

Many animals also redirect their activities to places where natural air conditioning exists. In the shade of dense forests, the temperature is often notice- ably lower than in open, sun-baked settings. Ravines and boulder-strewn edges of cliffs and ledges on north-

facing slopes can possess a microclimate that is markedly cooler than the ambient temperature, and underground burrows and rock cubbies in shady locations may have a temperature that is from 15 to 20 degrees lower than the air above. Con- sequently, life for the mice, voles, moles, and shrews which reside either on the ground or below its surface may remain unaffected by summer heat waves.

Although birds are limited to finding relief from the heat by retreating into the shade within or under trees, most species are far more tolerant of higher temperatures than are mammals. A chickadee, for example, normally maintains a body temperature of 105 degrees. A day with temperatures into the lower 90s is therefore more tolerable for this bird than it is for humans.

In order to prevent a build-up of metabolic heat within their bodies, all warm- blooded creatures, including humans, have various means of expelling excess heat from their systems. In the case of domestic dogs, coyotes, foxes, and black bears, air is rapidly passed over a moist tongue, which allows for evaporation much as sweat evaporates from a person's skin. Since there is a concentrated flow of blood in the tongue, any unwanted heat it carries can be quickly dissi- pated from the mouth of the animal.

A number of birds attempt to expel heat that is produced during food oxida- tion by rapidly pulling air into their throats, allowing for evaporation on special tissues inside their necks, and then expelling the heated vapor from their mouths. This is why some birds may be seen on hot days with their bills open while a fluttering movement may be observed in their throats.

In their attempt to radiate thermal energy to their surroundings, birds also greatly increase the flow of blood to their feet. Ordinarily a bird's feet do not allow for much blood flow, which effectively reduces heat loss during the colder months of the year. However, during hot weather, blood vessels in this part of the body become dilated, allowing for more heat to be dissipated through these extremities. In order to further cool itself, one species, the turkey vulture, is known to expel liquid wastes on its legs and feet. This provides for added heat loss through evaporation in these blood-filled appendages.

We humans may also note that more blood flows to our hands and feet when the weather is hot, as is evident by the swelling of these appendages, particularly fingers and toes.

Most wild creatures instinctively know what to do when the weather turns excessively hot. Perhaps this is why most people get that uncontrollable urge to visit the beach, eat ice cream, or simply relax inside on those days when a strong Bermuda high ushers in an air mass that is more typical of the Deep South than the Great North Woods.

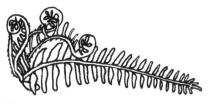

Blossoming Milkweed

The air in unmowed fields during mid-July routinely takes on a subtle sweet fragrance as milkweed comes into bloom. With the opening of the milkweed's spherical clusters of dark pink to light lavender-colored flowers, the appealing aroma of its nectar begins to spread to its surroundings. While sun-filled areas support a wide array of flowering plants, none produces as noticeable a scent at the height of summer as does the milkweed.

Like most other plants that grow in undisturbed parcels of open land, the milkweed is tall. Growing up to an inch per day, particularly when the weather turns hot, this native North American wildflower can grow to be four feet high by the time it is ready to bloom. Since competition for sunlight among the plants that crowd open areas is especially fierce, height is critically important for a plant to get the necessary exposure to the direct rays of the sun. The large leaves of the milkweed also help it absorb its fair share of light. These two features allow the milkweed to boost its own photosynthetic rate while reducing the light available to competing plants immediately around it.

Milkweed leaves, which are oval in shape, contain a fair quantity of nutrients. These would be gnawed on by most herbivores if not for the repugnant-tasting sap they contain. This sap, which is pure white and appears whenever a leaf or stem is damaged, gives milkweed its common name, and it is a telltale sign that helps distinguish milkweed from the many other forms of vegetation that grow in similar settings.

The caterpillar of the monarch butterfly is one of the very few forms of life that has the ability to consume the milkweed's relatively nutritious leaf fibers without being repulsed by the extremely acrid taste and glue-like texture of its sap. Because this insect ingests such large quantities of milkweed, it develops a similarly unappealing taste and is seldom eaten by other animals. Even during its adult stage, the monarch retains enough of this distasteful chemical

so that only butterfly predators on the verge of starvation would ever be inclined to kill and eat one of these bright orange- and black-winged bugs.

Centuries ago, many Native American tribes and early colonists were known to collect the shoots of the milkweed plant during May, when it is less than six inches in height. Once the milky sap was removed through repeated boiling, the newly forming leaves could be eaten, as they are quite tender, tasty, and nutritious during this stage of their development.

During late June and very early July, unopened flower clusters were gathered and cooked, and once the blossoms appeared, the nectar was collected because of its high sugar content. Although this task was exceedingly time consuming and tedious, the resulting fluid was said to be especially tasty and well worth the effort. Because the milkweed's flowers exude such sweet nectar, many insects are also attracted to them. Adult butterflies, wasps, flies, and bees may all be seen visiting its blossoms during this time of the summer.

Following pollination, the flowers eventually wither and a seed pod begins to form. Since this pod does not contain any of the milky fluid present in the leaves and stems of the plant, it was also harvested during the early stage of its development for use as a food.

Throughout the remainder of the summer, this uniquely-shaped pod grows until the hundreds of seeds inside are ready to be dispersed. Like the seeds of dandelions, milkweed seeds are very tiny and are connected to delicate, silk-like threads that enable them to be transported by the wind. Because these fibers are far more durable than the fragile fibers of dandelion seeds, milkweed seeds were once collected and used as stuffing in an assortment of items. During World War I, this fluffy material was extensively gathered and used as fill for life jackets.

Despite its rather common appearance, milkweed is a most noteworthy plant. It contributed in many ways to the civilizations that preceded ours, and today it has a very special place in the ecology of open areas in the North Country, where it provides a most refreshing aroma to the mid-July air.

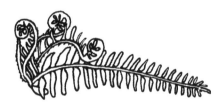

The Goldfinch

Due to the short spring and summer seasons in the North Country, all of our birds begin the process of breeding and nesting as early as possible, with the exception of one fairly common species. It is not until late June or early July that the goldfinch starts the activities involved in producing and raising its next generation of young.

With bright canary-yellow plumage covering most of its body, and its contrasting black wings, tail, and forehead patch, the male goldfinch is one of our most handsome small birds. Aside from its conspicuous coloration, this "wild canary" can also be identified in the air by its characteristic flight pattern. Rather than flying in a straight line, the goldfinch oscillates up and down, as if it were on a roller coaster. Additionally, as it flies – particularly on the up portion of each cycle – the bird utters a distinct, cheery call. This flight song, often composed of four quick notes, sounds like the bird is saying "per-chi-co-ree." Once this song is recognized, the goldfinch can be easily identified by its voice alone.

Like other finches, the goldfinch has a stout bill that is adapted for cracking open the hard covering of seeds. Plants like the ragweed and thistles that thrive in fields and meadows tend to form the bulk of its diet. Should these seeds become hard to find, the goldfinch will extend its search to brush-covered areas such as those along the shores of lakes and the edges of roads, golf course fairways, and ski trails. Because the goldfinch takes seeds that are placed in feeders, this bird is often seen around towns and villages regardless of the abundance or lack of natural foods in more favored locations.

Since dense forests do not support the type of plants that yield the seeds preferred by the wild canary, it is uncommon in the vast tracts of woodlands that cover much of northern New York. However, should a sizeable clearing exist in the wilderness, this perky-sounding bird may take up residence for the season. In places where it can access seeds throughout the winter, the goldfinch may be seen the year round. During the colder months, however, it may go unrecognized, as it supports drab, olive-colored plumage at that time of year.

Following the spring molt in early May, the male goldfinch develops its attractive breeding plumage. At this time, any small winter flocks that exist in an area disband, and individual mates establish their territories. In our region, it is during the weeks prior to Memorial Day when the male begins to proclaim ownership of a particular section of forest edge or meadow, periodically visiting selected perches in the area and bellowing out a warbling-twitter call that resembles the song of a canary. The male also reaffirms his claim to a certain parcel of land by occasionally flying around the perimeter of the area, often well above

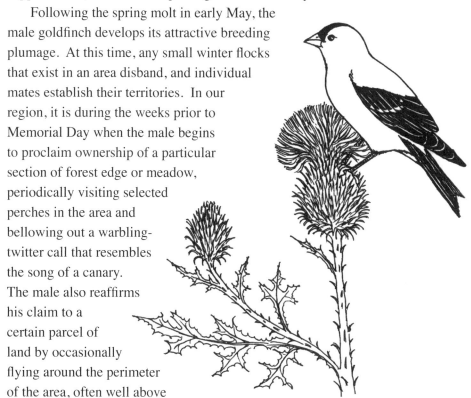

the tops of the trees, in an erratic and looping manner. A perceptive person may be able to get a fairly good idea of the location of a male's territory by closely observing him during these repeated solo flights. Each female then establishes a nesting territory in the spring within the boundaries of an area claimed by a male. Consequently, the pair that coexists in the same area eventually mates when the appropriate time arrives in early July.

Because of the goldfinches' late start in nesting, it is often not until mid-August that the nestlings develop the ability to fly. Because plant seeds favored by these birds do not fully mature until the latter part of summer, the fledglings are believed to have an easier time finding food than they might earlier in the season. Additionally, since many of these cold-hardy birds do not migrate, the all-too-quick end of summer that our region experiences does not seem to adversely affect their chances for survival. As a result, the goldfinches patiently wait to breed; they are perhaps the only birds that are still in the early to middle stages of their nesting season during mid-July.

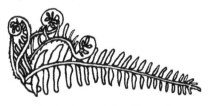

Molting Mallards

There aren't any birds in the North Country that are incapable of flight; however, around this time of the year, all ducks and geese in our region experience the loss of their flight feathers for a brief period, which temporarily renders them unable to fly.

The shedding of feathers, better known as molting, occurs in all birds; it is the necessary means by which old and worn plumage is periodically replaced. In most species of birds, the outer wing feathers that are fundamental for flight are not all lost at the same time. Rather, they are replaced in a specific sequence over a lengthy span of time, leaving enough flight feathers on the outer edge of its wing for the bird to maintain its ability to fly. Ducks and geese, however, experience a simultaneous shedding of all their flight feathers, which causes them to be grounded for several weeks until new ones grow in.

The time of the year when this event occurs varies greatly and depends on both the individual species as well as the sex of the bird. For the mallard, the male is the first to molt; he begins this process shortly after the end of the mating season, which is typically during mid-June in the North Country. At that time, the drake, which is the proper name for a male duck, initially loses the brightly-colored feathers on its head and body. The plumage that replaces it is drabber in color, and the drake is said to be in its eclipse, or non-breeding plumage, phase. The dull color supported by the drake makes it less conspicuous, which is vital for a bird that is soon to lose its primary means of escape. The feathers that form in early summer are also less dense, which allows the mallard to more effectively dissipate body heat.

Prior to shedding its flight feathers, a duck spends an increased amount of time feeding, in order to develop a layer of fat. Once its flying ability is lost, the bird tends to remain in hiding as much as possible. It seldom ventures into the open to feed, as doing so would expose it to the view of any nearby predator. This is why a male mallard which was regularly seen along some stretch of open lakeshore or marsh throughout the spring may temporarily disappear for a time during the early to mid-summer.

Because a female has young to care for, she retains her outer wing feathers much longer than does the drake. By the middle of August, her maturing chicks acquire the strength in their muscles and feathers on their wings that enable them

125

to finally leave the surface of the water and fly for short distances. Once they have developed this natural skill, the ducklings no longer need their mother to lure danger away, as they can simply take to the air when approached by a mink or bobcat. It is then that the hen molts. As is the case with the drake, the hen also tends to retreat to some out-of-the-way place in which to safely pass the time when she can only waddle along the shore or swim quickly through the weed-covered surface of a marsh.

During the latter part of the summer, the drake experiences a second molt involving only the plumage on its head and body. This molt results in the growth of feathers that are brighter in color and far more attractive to the eyes of a hen. Although it will be a while before most of these birds become involved with the process of pair formation, these individuals will possess the appropriate garb needed to catch the eye of a potential mate when that time comes.

All birds routinely shed their plumage at various times during the year, so finding a feather on the ground is not uncommon. In the case of the waterfowl, though, this summer occurrence temporarily leaves them in the same situation as the ostrich or penguin.

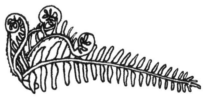

Fresh Water Mussels

You can often see thin, dark brown shells that are typically elongated in shape scattered sporadically along the shoreline of most aquatic settings. These are all that remain of a group of mollusks called fresh water mussels after they have been extracted from the bottom by one of several creatures that enjoy dining on their meaty interior.

In the North Country, there are numerous species of these flat-shelled invertebrates, and each one is adapted to function best under a very specific set of environmental conditions. The depth of the water, the material covering the bottom (muddy sediment, sand, gravel, stones, or rocks), and whether the water is flowing or not are all factors that determine which species is likely to occur in

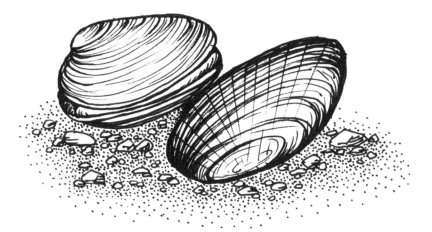

any given place. (The location of a shell on the shore may not reflect the type of setting from which the mussel was taken, however, as many animals move to the shore to open the shell after finding a mussel on the bottom.)

Like other bivalves, mussels get their nourishment by filtering the microorganisms that are suspended in the water. Those species that occur in rivers and streams rely on the natural flow along the bottom to push water through their partially opened shells. The mussels that inhabit lakes and ponds, where there is a lack of current, have evolved the ability to pump water through their body themselves. This allows the mussels to acquire food particles and to extract dissolved oxygen for respiration.

During the early summer, fresh water mussels enter into the reproductive stage of their complex life cycle. When the water warms to a certain temperature, males release sperm to their surroundings in an attempt to get this genetic material to nearby females or receptive individuals downstream. After fertilization, the eggs in the female begin a process of transformation into larvae, properly referred to as glochidia. In some species of mussels, the development stage of the glochidia within the female may be completed by late summer. In other species, the larvae will not be ready for release until late the following spring.

Once expelled, the glochidia must attach themselves within a day to the gills of a fish or they will die. Most species of mussels target a specific species of fish for this activity. During this stage, mussels become parasitic, feeding on the blood and gill tissue of the host fish in order to proceed with their development into adults. The females of various species of mussels have evolved some unique strategies for enticing a fish close enough to increase their offspring's chances of reaching a suitable host. (Although the tiny larvae are not believed to cause a fish any significant harm while clamped onto their gills, some species of fish have evolved strategies of their own to deal with this form of parasitism.)

Naturalists believe that the parasitic stage of fresh water mussels that occur in rivers and streams is related more to their need to be transported upstream than to the need for the animal protein acquired when attached to their host. Males are especially benefited when carried against the current, as occupying a place further up a flowing waterway increases the likelihood that their sperm will reach more females when released during their reproductive period.

After a period of time, the glochidia transform into small adults and fall from their hosts. Because the type of fish that serves as a host to the mussel usually shares the same habitat preference, the chances are good that a mussel will drop free and sink to an area on the bottom where conditions are favorable for its life as an adult. Once that happens, the young adult will partially bury itself in the substrate material and remain in the same general vicinity for the rest of its life. Even though a mussel has the ability to move short distances, most individuals seldom travel more than a few dozen yards during the course of a lifetime that can span many years.

Because fresh water mussels feed on matter contained in the water, their health is only as good as that of the aquatic system in which they reside. Also, since a mussel depends on a certain species of fish during a portion of its life, a decrease in the population of that variety of fish can result in a similar reduction in the number of mussels. These factors allow fresh water mussels to serve as bioindicators – organisms that reflect the general quality of their surrounding environment.

The shells of fresh water mussels can still be commonly found scattered about rocks and near logs along the shores of most waterways throughout the North Country. This indicates that the water in these areas still harbors a vibrant population of microscopic organisms, host fish remain plentiful, and predators such as the muskrat and otter that enjoy the taste of mussels as part of their meal continue to thrive in the region.

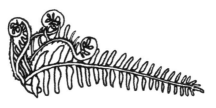

Earwigs

One of the numerous bugs that occur in and around North Country homes during the summer is the earwig, a rather grotesque insect that is difficult to mistake for any other form of invertebrate life. With its set of long, fierce-looking pincers that extend from the tip if its abdomen, this dark brown insect, which averages three-quarters to one inch in length, has a uniquely menacing form. The body of an earwig is coated with a hard, dense material, much like a beetle, yet despite this rigid appearance, the earwig exhibits a remarkable degree of flexibility. Also like a beetle, the earwig has wings that are impossible to notice, except when it is ready to take to the air or immediately after it has landed, but because it seldom flies, these short wings are rarely seen. The earwig is also characterized by a body that can be flattened. This feature, coupled with its flexibility, allows the earwig to squeeze and wiggle its way into various cracks and crevices which conceal its presence during the day.

Being strictly nocturnal, the earwig is most often seen after being uncovered from a daytime retreat. Damp places are preferred as hiding spots. This draws the earwig under boxes, crates, and other items that are located on garage and basement floors. Nooks and crannies among the boards used in and around decks, porches, and patios are other favored locations where the earwig hides, as are small chunks of bark and pieces of woody mulch set out in flower beds, the soft soil in flower boxes, and areas of lawn in which the grass is thick.

After dusk, earwigs emerge into the open to forage for whatever is available. A perfect example of an omnivore, the earwig consumes a wide variety of both plant and animal matter, including very small invertebrates such as aphids and mites. The forcep-like appendages on its abdomen are used to help subdue even sizeable bugs which it encounters and wishes to eat. If it is able to, the earwig will also scavenge and eat any bits and pieces of dead animal matter it happens to find. Algae, mold, and the leaves of some plants are commonly included in

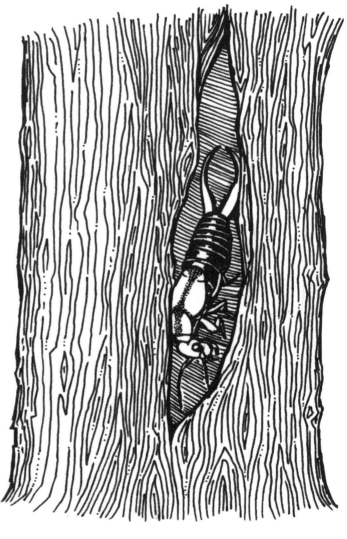

the earwig's diet, and in gardens, this insect is known to gnaw on the leaves and petals of flowers such as marigolds and roses. Occasionally, homeowners will blame the slug for damage to the foliage of lettuce and the blossoms of plants in flower beds and porch boxes. While this slimy, shell-less mollusk is responsible for chewing the leaves and petals of numerous cultivated plants, the earwig may share some of the blame.

Although the earwig is nocturnal, like some moths and the June bug, it is drawn to areas where there is artificial light. Walkways lined with lamps and areas illuminated by porch lights, street lights, and flood lights are all places in which the earwig will concentrate its foraging activities.

In areas where their presence is deemed unacceptable, the earwig population can be easily lured into traps and removed with relatively little effort. A stack of slightly-crumpled pieces of cardboard or wads of rolled-up newspaper that have been moistened ever so slightly and placed in a protected spot are the type of shelter into which the earwig will readily retreat during the day, and flakes of oatmeal, bread crumbs, or shredded cheese can be used to lure the earwig to the front of such traps. In the morning, one can simply pick up the cardboard or paper and empty out all the earwigs. By doing this on successive nights for a week or two, most of the earwigs from that immediate area can be captured.

Eliminating earwigs, however, may allow aphids, mites, and other tiny, pesky invertebrates to flourish. Although the earwig is often viewed as an ugly, unwanted pest, it does have an important place in nature, although most people maintain that its rightful place is away from their home.

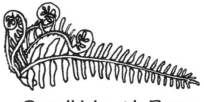

Small Mouth Bass

While some species of animal life are able to function quite well under a wide variety of environmental conditions, others can't, and the small mouth bass is one that cannot. Known to anglers for its strength and feistiness when hooked, and to fish-eating enthusiasts for its fine-tasting meat, the small mouth bass is known to fisheries' biologists for its sensitivity to changing aquatic conditions in lakes and rivers.

After the ice thaws during the mid-spring, the small mouth bass returns to an active existence. As the water warms, this popular game fish seeks out a gravel-bottomed area in which the water is clear and rich in dissolved oxygen. In the North Country, rivers as well as many lakes provide a suitable habitat in which this fish can spawn once the water reaches at least sixty degrees, which typically is not until the last few weeks of spring.

Once thermal conditions become acceptable, a female will lay several thousand eggs in a nest that was constructed by the male. In order for these eggs to successfully hatch and for the fry to develop into small bass, the water temperature in the nesting site must remain in the sixty-degree range. Should a persistent period of unseasonably cold weather significantly lower the water's temperature, most, if not all, of the eggs and recently-hatched fry will perish.

A reduction in water clarity can also be lethal to nesting success. An outbreak of intense thunderstorms accompanied by torrential rains can cause enough sand and silt to be picked up and temporarily suspended to cloud the water beyond an acceptable limit. Even moderate rains can wash enough fertilizers and pesticides into aquatic systems to temporarily contaminate the water around a bass spawning site, resulting in its destruction.

When aquatic conditions deteriorate for whatever reason, even for a short span of time, the number of young bass that survive will be minimal, regardless of the number of spawning adults. However, when conditions are ideal, a single pair of bass may be able to successfully produce hundreds, if not thousands, of offspring.

As summer approaches and the water warms, the newly-spawned small mouth bass moves into cooler areas of the lake or river. Unlike other members of the sunfish family to which it belongs, the small mouth bass prefers settings in which the water temperature remains in the sixties. In lakes, this temperature is maintained in deeper areas, especially where there are rocks and other submerged items scattered along the bottom for this predator to hide behind.

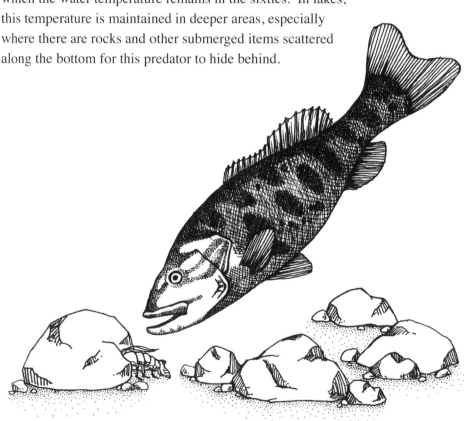

In flowing water, the bass may move into deep holes, areas that are further upriver, and stretches of water that are covered with shade. Additionally, to further insure that its body won't become warmer than the water, the small mouth bass tends to avoid exposure to the sun, especially on clear days when its rays are exceptionally intense. During such cloudless weather, this fish often forages for prey in the early morning or late afternoon hours. When the skies are overcast, or when it is rainy, the small mouth bass may go in search of food anytime during the day.

Despite its name, this aquatic predator has a sizeable mouth that is capable of swallowing some fairly large creatures. Crayfish that come out from under rocks, frogs that swim too far from the shore, and smaller fish that venture from the safety of the shallows are all regularly gulped down by the bass. The insects that reside in the various settings inhabited by the bass also form a fair portion of its diet.

Bass feed actively throughout the summer and will relocate periodically whenever conditions warrant. As the water cools in late summer and into the autumn, they begin to migrate toward their wintering areas. Unlike trout, perch, and pike, the small mouth bass lapses into a lethargic state toward the end of the autumn, so this fish must retreat to a spot where there is virtually no current. While this is seldom a problem in a lake, bass often must swim many miles in order to find an appropriate site in a river.

One major environmental factor that small mouth bass are extremely sensitive to is the water's pH. As a general rule, as the acid concentration increases, the health of the bass decreases. While the North Country is well known for its abundance of pristine waterways, acid rain has impacted the population of this fish in some areas. When an abundance of small mouth bass exist in an area, it is rewarding not only to anglers, but also to individuals who want to preserve the health and well-being of this region.

August

Perch

It is not unusual or difficult to catch a perch, whether you're fishing in a deep lake or a shallow pond. Although during the spring, this tough-scaled, spiny-rayed fish often teases the trout angler by continually nibbling on his line and occasionally stealing his bait, by mid-summer, individuals fishing for bass or pike all too often end up snagging more perch than their targeted species.

With its yellowish-orange underside and the dark green, finger-like stripes that reach down its side, the perch is fairly attractive. In addition to this distinctive coloration, the perch can be identified because it has two separate fins on its back rather than one. As is also the case with the walleye, the front dorsal fin of the perch is supported by very sharp spines, while the rear dorsal fin contains much softer and more flexible rays.

Because of its colorful appearance, slim shape, tough scales, and bony fins, the perch is sometimes falsely grouped with sunfish and bass. These two fish belong to a closely-related but separate family whose members are characterized by a single, elongated dorsal fin.

While the perch remains active during the winter, as any ice fisherman will surely attest, this fish has a distinct preference for warm water. Experiments performed in research aquariums and data collected from northern lakes show that mature perch prefer a temperature close to seventy degrees. In most North Country lakes during the summer, such thermal conditions frequently exist from the surface to nearly ten feet down. Although adult perch thrive in this temperature, they do not confine their activities to it, and they frequently stray into cooler waters when searching for food.

Yearling perch, which average from two to three inches in length, and the fry that hatch from eggs laid in late April and early May have been found to favor waters that are slightly warmer. Consequently, these individuals tend to spend more time in the shallow waters closer to shore. Since there is normally more vegetation in these areas, these smaller fish can hide among the weeds, which protect them from heavy predation by a variety of aquatic creatures. And yet it has been estimated by one researcher that only one in every 5,000 perch ever makes it to the age of one.

Shallow, weedy areas are also sought out by young perch because these settings tend to be richer in food. For their first year of life, perch feed almost exclusively on the countless microscopic animals that exist in such aquatic settings. During their second and third years, the bulk of their diet is composed of the various invertebrates that also thrive in shallow places.

At the age of three, perch mature into adults, although, unlike mammals and birds, perch (and other fish) continue to grow throughout their lives, which average from seven to ten years in this section of the country. As they get older and larger, their diet gradually shifts to small fish, including their own kind.

In bodies of water in which natural predators and anglers fail to reduce the

numbers of perch, large schools can develop. Such large numbers of perch, each with a voracious appetite, will lead to a dramatic reduction in the population of all the small fish in that area.

After eliminating much of their own food source, perch then fall prey to tiny, parasitic worms which infest their flesh. The resultant decrease in nutrients stunts the growth of perch and eventually, of numerous other game fish that rely on small fish as a principle source of food. Inevitably, unchecked perch populations have a serious negative impact on the size and health of native trout.

While small forage fish are strongly preferred by older perch, they are not the sole items in their diet. Regardless of their size and age, perch continue to scour the bottom and the surface of the water for bugs. During the summer, a school of perch may churn up a small section of a quiet lake as they dine on a recent hatch of flies. Their willingness to consume anything from worms, to tiny crayfish, to chunks of cut bait is the characteristic that allows them to be so easily caught. Unlike game fish, perch seldom exhibit finicky eating habits. This is much to the dismay of the serious angler, but a delight to the youngsters who catch them and to those many people with a taste for the perch's flavorful flesh.

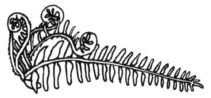

The Garter Snake

For many people, there is nothing as traumatic as looking down and seeing a snake. While the chance of encountering one of these limbless reptiles in the North Country is relatively low, the probability is high that when one is sighted, it will be an eastern garter snake.

Garter (not garden) snakes form a group of reptiles that are recognized by three yellowish stripes on their back that run the length of their slender bodies. Of the two species present in the North Country, the eastern garter snake is the more common and the one that is likely to venture into the open during the day and be seen by people. Although its coloration varies from one individual to another, this species can be identified by the dark checkered pattern that fills the area between its three yellow stripes. In this geographic region, most adult garter snakes range in length from fourteen to twenty-two inches and are not much bigger around than a person's index finger.

The eastern garter snake is more widespread than any other snake throughout the Adirondacks, as it is likely to be found in places where there is a fair amount of ground cover. Areas of thick grass and weeds, especially if there are loose and cracked rocks or fallen logs and limbs, are particularly inviting to this snake. Such settings help to conceal its presence from its many natural enemies and offer rich supplies of food. Crickets, grasshoppers, worms, salamanders, and small toads are the main items in the garter snake's diet.

The garter snake uses its keen sense of smell to track down several of the creatures on which its preys. The earthworm, for example, is known to emit a specific chemical as it undulates its way across the soil's surface. By following this trail, the garter snake may get close enough to see its quarry. Once it comes within eyesight, the garter snake rapidly closes in and strikes at its victim. There is some evidence that the saliva of this snake contains a very weak poison which acts only on lower forms of life, especially amphibians. The garter snake does not pose any danger to humans, unless you have salamander blood flowing

through your body.

Nooks and crannies within the garter snake's habitat provide places into which it can retreat when thermal conditions become unfavorable. Since snakes are cold blooded, they are unable to regulate their body temperature by internal processes. As a result, all species that inhabit northern climates must seek out places that retain some heat during cool nights, such as rocks that have baked in the sun during the day. Cracks and crevices can also serve as a refuge on those occasions when the sun elevates the temperature of the soil's surface above ninety degrees. The garter snake functions best when the temperature of its surroundings is in the sixties and seventies.

The ribbon snake is another species of garter snake that occurs in the North Country. It seems to favor damper sites, such as those near ponds, lakes, and rivers, and it is less likely to sit in the open for any length of time. The ribbon snake is characterized by the more uniform color of the dark lines that run on its back between its yellow stripes. Also, the ribbon snake has a much longer tail than that of any other species of garter snake.

Although snakes appear as if they are nothing but tail, all of these creatures are said to have this appendage emerging from the end of their body. On the underside of a snake, the tail begins just beyond its anal opening, at the point between where the single row of belly scales ends and multiple rows of scales begin. The belly scales are those skin structures that are used to grasp surface irregularities and help this creature in its unusual process of locomotion. (These are relatively fragile, so handling a live snake should be done with great care to avoid injuring it.)

Unlike most other snakes, garter snakes do not lay eggs; rather, they bear their young alive. This atypical process of reptilian birth occurs in our region during the month of August. The number of babies that the female bears averages around two dozen, although this number can vary greatly. Like the young of other snakes, the newborns are not dependent on their mother for either food or protection, thus they stray away from their parent shortly after being born.

In our region, all species of snakes can be identified by carefully noting an individual's color and markings. Chances are that most snakes seen in the Adirondacks will be garter snakes.

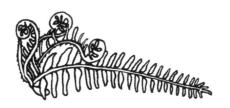

Blossoming Goldenrod

There are times in nature when a single form of vegetation becomes more conspicuous than any of the other forms of plant life in an area. During the month of August, in open, unmowed places such as beneath power lines, along the side of railroad right-of-ways, and in seldom-grazed pastures and undisturbed meadows, goldenrod becomes such a visibly dominant component of the North Country environment. With sizeable sprays of yellow composite flowers topping its tall stalks and its ability to develop into extensive patches, this native North American plant is difficult to overlook.

While goldenrod may appear to be one specific type of plant, especially when a field of it is seen through the window of a car, there are actually many dozens of different species that grow in this geographic region. Each has adapted to flourish in slightly different sunlight and soil conditions, but they all produce the same yellow-colored flowers during August.

Aside from giving open areas a familiar yellowish tint, this group of plants is also responsible for providing food to many creatures. The arching plumes of delicate flowers that these so-called weeds bear secrete nectar that is sought by various bugs. This is why an assortment of bees, butterflies, and other insects may be seen flying about areas containing goldenrod in bloom. Since many sources of nectar begin to dwindle during the second half of summer, the sweet fluid of goldenrod often becomes the sole source of food to small, sugar-craving creatures. However, while goldenrod's flowers yield sought-after nectar, they fail to release much of a detectable aroma to their surroundings. This is why traveling past an area laden with blossoming goldenrod is never as appealing to one's sense of smell as passing by a thicket of lilacs in late May, or a field of milkweed during mid-July.

Goldenrod flowers are also known for producing an abundance of pollen that is rich in protein. Additionally, its sticky texture and relatively large size, as far as pollen goes, makes it easier for various invertebrates to collect. When it's observed while visiting a stalk of goldenrod, a bee may be noticed extracting the nectar with its tongue, then pushing tiny wads of this powdery material into the sacs on its hind legs.

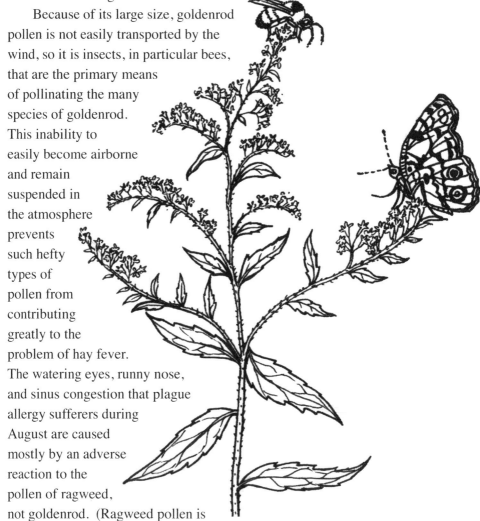

Because of its large size, goldenrod pollen is not easily transported by the wind, so it is insects, in particular bees, that are the primary means of pollinating the many species of goldenrod. This inability to easily become airborne and remain suspended in the atmosphere prevents such hefty types of pollen from contributing greatly to the problem of hay fever. The watering eyes, runny nose, and sinus congestion that plague allergy sufferers during August are caused mostly by an adverse reaction to the pollen of ragweed, not goldenrod. (Ragweed pollen is very tiny and nicely designed to be carried for miles. Its microscopic size also enables it to more easily penetrate and aggravate the lining of a person's respiratory system.) Since ragweed is rather nondescript, its presence often goes overlooked in the open places where it grows. Goldenrod, which typically grows alongside ragweed, is the plant that is most often noted and, therefore, has come to be associated with the ill effects of this late summer medical condition.

Yet while goldenrod is seldom responsible for causing an allergic reaction, it is not totally innocent in the overall hay fever scene. Open areas that favor the growth of ragweed and goldenrod are also ideal places for tree seeds to sprout and take root. This is why it usually doesn't take long for seedling and saplings to reclaim a logged-over area and convert it back to its former wooded state. Once goldenrod becomes well established on a site, however, it is known to greatly hamper this process of successional change. By manufacturing a chemical that is toxic to trees and shrubs, goldenrod prevents the shady conditions of a developing forest which would be fatal to it and ragweed. Consequently, a meadow of goldenrod is likely to remain a meadow of goldenrod for many years, thereby enabling ragweed to continue to flourish.

While the North Country is best known for its vast tracts of wilderness forests and pristine lakes, there are also some incredibly beautiful meadows that exist within the region. Certainly, a hike to the summit of one of the High Peaks is an unforgettable experience, yet a stroll through an uncut meadow maintained solely by the many species of goldenrod that grow there can be equally uplifting, especially during August. That is, provided you don't have hay fever, in which case you would be better off spending all of your time basking in the sun in the middle of some lake.

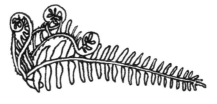

The Yellow-Bellied Sapsucker

Most animals do not draw attention to themselves when foraging, as they produce very little, if any, sound when searching for food. Woodpeckers, however, are an exception to this rule. As they tap tree trunks, chisel away pieces of bark, and chip out chunks of wood, they create enough noise to alert any individual who is tuned in to the sounds of nature to their presence.

In the North Country, one common, yet often unrecognized, member of this

141

family of hard-billed birds is the yellow-bellied sapsucker. While this bird is regularly seen by people who spend time out-of-doors, especially in forested settings, few are able to identify it as a sapsucker.

Like the majority of its relatives, the yellow-bellied sapsucker supports black-and-white plumage that creates a checkered or laddered pattern over several areas of its body, especially on its back and tail. It also has a patch of red on its head, possesses the general body shape of most woodpeckers, and exhibits the same habit of latching onto the side of trees, rather than perching on a limb as most other birds do. And like that of the downy and hairy woodpeckers, the underside of the sapsucker is off-white, not yellow, as its name would imply. In fact, while it does have a tinge of amber along the sides of its breast, this subtle color feature is easily overlooked.

The most prominent characteristic of the yellow-bellied sapsucker – and the best way to identify it – is the large white patch across the middle of its wing. Also, the red patch on this bird's head is situated on its forehead, as opposed to the top and back as in other woodpeckers. (The male sapsucker has a corresponding red patch on its upper throat, while the female's is white. This color difference can be used to tell the sexes apart.)

Rows of small holes drilled into healthy trees are the telltale sign that a sapsucker is in an area. Other woodpeckers ordinarily tear away pieces of a tree's surface and dig out small cavities in a trunk or branch in an effort to obtain bugs. The sapsucker is the only one that pecks several rows of shallow holes that are just deep enough to tap into the soft, inner sections of the bark. It is through this conductive tissue that woody plants carry most of their nutrient-enriched sap. Once the bark is punctured, it doesn't take long for the sap to begin oozing out and collecting in these wells. Like the hummingbird, the sapsucker is equipped with a long tongue that is adapted for lapping up these tiny drops of liquid.

After a sapsucker leaves its drilling site, it is quite common for a host of bugs to assemble there to take advantage of the flowing sap. By periodically returning to the tree, the sapsucker not only has the opportunity to lick up the sap that has dripped out, but also gets the chance to consume the bugs that have happened upon the scene.

In fact, some naturalists believe that the primary reason for creating these wells is for the bugs they lure, rather than the sap which they yield. Regardless, the sapsucker laps up any sap that collects in these holes and is known to drive away other creatures, such as the hummingbird and red squirrel, which are also attracted to it. As it makes its way around its territory, the yellow-bellied sapsucker also visits dead trees for the bugs which may be present on their surfaces.

The damage the sapsucker inflicts on trees is only minor. Healing begins as the summer commences and rows of scars eventually replace the wells used by this bird. In a year or two these scars fade, causing the record of the bird's presence to disappear. It is the fresh wells and the not-yet-healed scars from old feeding activities that are evidence of the abundance of sapsuckers in our region.

In another month, as the flow of sap in trees gradually decreases, the yellow-bellied sapsucker begins to migrate from our forests to woodlands in more southern regions. Until then, it is wise not to be too hasty in labeling a black-and-white bird that is clinging to the side of a tree and rapping its sharp-pointed beak into the bark as "merely" a woodpecker. In the North Country, there is a chance that the feathery creature that has caught your attention is none other than the famed yellow-bellied sapsucker.

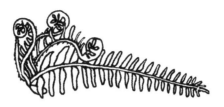

Fall Web Worms

It is ordinarily during early August when thin translucent sheets of delicate white fibers begin to sporadically appear on an outer twig or two of various trees and shrubs across the North Country. These rather unsightly veils, which engulf the leaves at the end of a branch, seem to pull the foliage into a more concentrated cluster. A close examination of this massive cocoon-like structure reveals the presence of numerous hairy caterpillars that can vary in size depending on the exact time of the season. These are fall web worms, which are the larvae of a seldom-noticed species of tiger moth.

Earlier during the summer, the adult laid its egg mass on a preferred species of deciduous tree or shrub such as a cherry or willow. Semi-open areas are especially favored sites, for these locations typically contain leaves that receive a healthy amount of sunlight and are particularly lush, yet they have enough shade to allow more favorable temperatures to be maintained within the loosely formed tent on clear, cloudless days.

After the eggs hatch, dozens of tiny caterpillars begin to chew on the leaves in the immediate area on the host tree. While they are meandering about, these larvae leave behind delicate threads that quickly form into a web-like covering over that particular section of the tree. As these immature insects grow in size, they gradually expand their feeding area and may incorporate one or several adjacent twigs into their swelling encampment.

The communal nest that is formed helps to insulate the occupants against the cool nights that can frequently occur as summer begins to wane. It also serves as a moisture barrier during rainy periods and against the heavy dew that regularly forms at this time of the year.

The tent-like enclosure of the fall web worm also helps to conceal its presence from the numerous creatures that prey on caterpillars. Because of the safety afforded by this silken structure, fall web worms are reluctant to leave it for any length of time, although they will periodically emerge in order to travel to nearby leaf clusters when it becomes necessary to enlarge their communal nest. They may also temporarily vacate this sanctuary on especially hot, sunny days when there is little breeze, for the temperature inside may become intolerably hot.

The hairy texture of this and other caterpillars is believed to make fall web worms unappealing as a meal to some birds. Others, however, are quick to devour this furry insect should it be seen undulating along a section of twig. While many birds overlook these white masses of web and encapsulated leaves when foraging for insects, a few have learned that they contain a rich supply of bugs. The yellow warbler is reported to target these colonies of caterpillars and can quickly decimate web worm numbers when it takes up residence in an area.

It takes the caterpillar a little over a month to reach the stage when it is ready to pupate. Just before this point in its development is reached, the web worm abandons its nest and strikes out to find a sheltered place in which to spend the winter. A cluster of dead leaves next to a rock, soft soil under a rotting log, or a pile of fallen twigs and decomposing bark in a sheltered hollow are all places to which this caterpillar will retreat. It then spins a cocoon around itself and enters

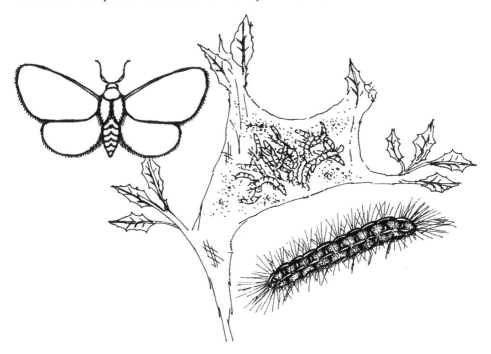

into a period of dormancy that lasts until mid-spring. After the weather turns warm again, the pupa transforms into an adult and finally emerges as early summer arrives.

While the communal tent produced by the web worm closely resembles the structure produced by the tent caterpillar, these two insects should not be confused with one another. The tent caterpillars make a shelter which is always located in the crotch of a tree or around an inner branch that is forked, rather than toward the end of a single twig. Additionally, the fall web worm seldom leaves its shelter to feed, as the foliage which serves as its source of food is enclosed within its tent. Since there are never any leaves inside a tent caterpillar's shelter, this gnawing bug is forced to exit its shelter during the day to forage for food. The tent caterpillar also becomes active shortly after the leaves erupt from the buds during the late spring. By the time the fall web worm begins to establish its tent, the tent caterpillar has abandoned its shelter and is well on its way to becoming an adult.

The sight of a large white sheet of fine threads is not uncommon in the North Country. These structures are particularly abundant in areas disturbed by human settlement, where cherry and willow trees are more likely to grow. While the tent caterpillar is responsible for some of these insect houses, the web worm is the bug that created those that are seen engulfing the ends of twigs during fall in the North Country.

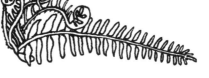

Wild Black Cherry

Among the native trees that commonly grow throughout the North Country, only the wild black cherry yields a tiny yet juicy, uniquely-flavored fruit that may be harvested for human consumption. Toward the end of August, around the same time as uneaten raspberries are dropping to the ground, the small clusters of fruit that dangle from the ends of wild black cherry twigs begin to ripen. These pea-size cherries, which are green throughout the summer, form in clusters on short stalks lying along an elongated, two-inch main strand, creating what is known as a raceme. While nearly the entire cherry is composed of a hard pit, properly called a stone, there is a thin layer of tissue surrounding the interior seed that develops a juicy texture with an appealing taste. As the fruit ripens, its initial green transforms into a burgundy color and finally into a deep purple to true black that indicates it is ready to harvest.

Although people seldom collect wild black cherries, many forms of wildlife are drawn to areas containing cherry trees, as their berries are a valuable source of food to both herbivores and omnivores alike. Animals ranging in size from songbirds, mice, and voles, to raccoons, deer, and bears all depend upon this crop of fruit from late August through mid-September, and occasionally beyond. And in turn, cherry trees depend on wildlife, for they help with the process of seed dispersal. The pit at the center of a cherry has a dense covering that is impervious to the digestive juices of all creatures. As a bird or a bear eats the fruit, it also swallows the pit, which passes through its intestines completely intact. Eventually, this seed is eliminated from the animal, usually some distance away from where it was consumed, and hopefully, in an area favorable for seed development.

Because the wild black cherry is a tree that requires a substantial amount of direct sunlight for growth, stands of cherries normally occur in areas in which the canopy has been opened and young trees are beginning to develop. Disturbances

such as ice storms, wind damage, disease, and logging operations all help to create favorable sunlight conditions for the wild black cherry.

However, open areas, although favorable for the growth of older saplings and mature trees, are not ideal for seed germination. Cherry seeds require consistently moist soil conditions for sprouting and seedling development, and open areas tend to be too dry. Additionally, these settings frequently contain plants like asters and goldenrod, which emit chemicals to the soil that are toxic to this cherry, and the meadow vole is known to griddle the bark of the saplings during harsh winters. It is partially- to mostly-wooded settings, where the ground is covered with a layer of dead leaves, twigs, and rotting bark (rather than grasses and weeds), that are most favorable for seed germination and growth.

When an opening occurs in the canopy above, the sapling quickly responds and grows into the space, often out-competing the saplings of other tree species for that spot. In cases where a break in the canopy fails to form, the young tree will slowly die from a lack of direct sunlight.

By selectively cutting a forest, favorable light conditions can be created for the wild black cherry. Because of its hard and durable wood and its attractive color and grain design, wild black cherry lumber is one of the most valuable commodities our woodlands have to offer.

As it grows, a cherry tree develops a defense system to prevent attack by certain herbivores. The sap of this tree contains a chemical that yields a cyanide compound when exposed to the air. Should its leaves become wilted or damaged by insects or other small organisms, these structures will form a highly toxic substance to discourage any continued attack. Healthy foliage, however, may be eaten without ill effects, as long as it's consumed quickly. This is how a deer or varying hare may gulp down several wild black cherry leaves and not be adversely impacted. The meadow vole, porcupine, and beaver are all known to gnaw on the bark of the wild black cherry during the late fall and winter after the sap has drained from the tree, but this outer woody tissue is avoided during the spring and summer, times when there is a much higher concentration of sap and cyanide in it.

Although there are other species of cherries that commonly grow in the North Country, none produce the high quality wood or the unique tasting fruit of the wild black cherry. Choke cherries may be eaten in limited numbers when they ripen, but their fruit has an unappealing bitter quality – hence their name. If a person wishes to produce a flavorful jam or jelly, or a spirit with a taste that is different from any wine, then wild black cherries should be the cherry of choice.

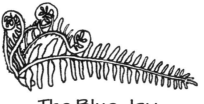

The Blue Jay

Late summer is normally a quiet time for birds. Vocalizations are regularly used throughout the spring breeding season as part of courtship rituals and during the early to mid-summer nesting period for maintaining a claim to a particular territory. With the arrival of August and the abandonment of their nests and breeding territories, however, most birds become silent. But in the North Country there are a handful of species that continue to produce calls, and of these, the blue jay vies for the title of loudest and noisiest "songster."

Young blue jays are slow to develop, and the young continue to depend upon both parents to provide them with food until early autumn. By repeatedly squawking, the fledglings are able to announce their hunger, and adult blue jays act quickly to appease the fledglings' cries for food. Caterpillars, spiders, grasshoppers, crickets, beetles, and miscellaneous bugs, all staples of their early diet, are rich in animal protein, which is essential at this stage of their growth for building appropriate body tissues.

As summer wanes and the fledglings' physical development nears completion, fruits and berries become a more important part of their diet. This coincides with the ripening of the raspberries, blackberries, wild black cherries and other assorted seeds that occur throughout the region. It's a noisy time, with the fledglings' crying for food and their parents responding in their attempt to draw the young birds to those places where suitable vegetable matter is abundant.

It is common during the late summer for several families of blue jays to congregate and merge into a more sizeable flock in thickets rich in berries or near trees laden with cherries. Their need to maintain contact with the other members of the flock, especially in places where the vegetation obscures their view, serves as yet another cause to vocalize. Not only do calls maintain the birds' knowledge of others' whereabouts, but these calls are also believed to communicate information regarding food availability and the presence of intruders.

The blue jay is a wary bird that is reluctant to forage in places where large animals or humans are present, or where a natural enemy, such as a fisher, bobcat, or domestic cat, is lurking. A person who happens into a thicket in which a flock of blue jays is foraging is guaranteed to set off a series of raucous calls.

During late August, as cultivated crops are being harvested, flocks of blue jays spend an increasing amount of time picking through the stubble for any edible matter that remains on the ground. Later in the autumn, acorns ripen and the blue jay shifts its attention to these large, meaty masts of the oaks. In temperate areas to our south, where oaks dominate the forests, acorns are reported to be the number one item in the blue jay's autumn and winter diet. In the North Country, where only scattered stands of oaks occur in the larger valleys and virtually none of these hardwoods exist at higher elevations, the blue jay is forced to find an alternate source of food that will last through the winter, or to migrate to an area where oaks are present.

Those individuals that resort to migration typically assemble into loosely organized flocks that can number into the hundreds.

Flocks of blue jays are difficult to detect, partly because of their silence when traveling, but also because they do not bunch together when in flight.

It may take several seconds after a single blue jay is seen flying above a forest clearing or over the tops of the trees around a house before another individual is noted, followed a short time later by another. Such a drawn-out assemblage may continue for many minutes before the last bird goes by.

Blue jays that remain in the North Country over winter tend to be older birds that have learned where bird feeders stocked with cracked corn and sunflower seeds are located. It is rare for a blue jay to be found in a wilderness area during the winter. Birds that are seen in remote locations at that time of year are often those that are resourceful enough to follow the wanderings of a pack of coyotes in a deer yard. These blue jays depend heavily on the scraps they can glean from periodic kills made by these predators.

When spring arrives and seeds and bugs can be picked up from the ground, blue jays return to populate the region. The arrival of the breeding season causes them to exercise their vocal talents once again, which draws attention to this handsome bird with the conspicuous crested head.

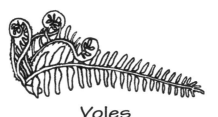

Voles

Late summer is the time when the population of most small rodents reaches its peak, and in many settings throughout the North Country, voles are the critters that top the list of most abundant mammals.

Looking very much like mice, voles are rodents that are characterized, in part, by a short, stubby tail, rather than one that is roughly equal in length to that of their body. Voles also possess smaller, less prominent ears than do mice, and their eyes are not as large and do not seem to protrude as much from their heads. In addition, voles have a snout that seems slightly more rounded in shape and less pointed when compared to the head of a mouse. Should a neighborhood cat leave a dead specimen on the porch or front step, the facial features of a vole may be noted in greater detail; otherwise, its short tail is its most obvious identifying feature.

Voles maintain a life that is more confined to the ground or just below the soil's surface than that of mice, which frequently climb. In areas where a dense growth of grasses, weeds, and small shrubs occur, voles often create runways through the thick vegetation by gnawing at the close clusters of shoots and stems. Voles are also known to utilize tunnels just below the surface to venture about their territory.

Because of their occasional subterranean tendencies, voles are sometimes confused with moles. Moles, however, are not rodents, seldom come to the surface, and feed almost entirely on invertebrate matter, while voles spend only a fraction of their time below the ground and are primarily herbivores.

Like mice, voles feed on whatever plant matter is seasonally available. During this season, berries and assorted seeds form the bulk of their diet. As the various crops of wild fruits diminish, mature seeds from trees and certain herbaceous plants become their staple food. Eventually, during the latter part of autumn, as these items become increasingly scarce, voles concentrate on fungal threads and tubers which can be extracted from the frozen ground. When these items become difficult to obtain, voles are known to gnaw on the bark of certain shrubs and saplings. As spring returns, tender sprouting greens become their food of choice.

Unlike mice, voles do not create scattered caches of food for use in winter. Since they are more inclined to prowl for food in nooks and crannies on the ground, such as in hollows below moss-covered rocks, in crevices between rocks, and in spaces under piles of leaves and dried weeds where snow does not accumulate, voles are not as adversely impacted by winter weather as are mice. Also, because of their ability to access the root system of certain plants, voles are less inclined to experience a loss of food in winter than are many other rodents.

The ability of a vole to get below ground and gnaw on tubers often gets this animal into trouble with gardeners who plant flowers like tulips and crocuses. Since flower bulbs contain a considerable store of nutrients, voles will consume them whenever they get the chance. Consequently, once a vole discovers a bed of such cultivated plants, the location will be visited regularly whenever a meal is needed.

As its name implies, the meadow vole is a resident of open settings, such as pastures, abandoned fields, and brushy areas. Despite being rarely seen, the meadow vole is often the most abundant mammal to occupy such open areas. This common vole is identified primarily by its nearly uniform dark gray fur. The red-backed vole is browner in color and has a rusty-tan stripe on its back that extends from its head to its tail, and this distinguishes it from other species. The red-backed vole inhabits heavily wooded areas, especially those in which the ground is slightly damp and where moss abounds on the forest floor. In stands of conifers that dominate the upper elevation of the Adirondacks, this vole may outnumber mice and rank as that setting's most common mammal.

Like mice, voles have a high reproductive rate which allows them to maintain large populations despite incredibly high losses due to predation. Nearly every terrestrial predator is known to hunt voles, and their abundance from mid-summer through the mid-autumn is the reason that many young carnivores are successful in making kills despite their inexperience at hunting. In this way, voles are instrumental in ensuring the ecological success of many larger forms of animal life.

The extremely shy and secretive nature of voles prevents them from being easily seen by humans. Predators, however, are quick to learn their ways and become experts at locating and snagging these small, meaty rodents. In spite of that, the nearly continuous breeding season which voles experience from early spring through the end of autumn allows them to maintain both their population and their ranking as one of the North Country's most prolific animals.

September

Hummingbirds Begin To Migrate

Coinciding with the exodus of summer vacationers from their seasonal camps and the return of children to school is the migration of hummingbirds from northern New York to more southern latitudes. It is around Labor Day in the North Country when dwindling daylight and cooler temperatures result in a reduction in the number of flowers that are in bloom. The corresponding decrease in the amount of available nectar, an essential source of food to these tiny iridescent creatures, causes them to head to areas in which summer is still well entrenched.

The adult males are the first to leave, as they build up necessary fat deposits sooner than either adult females or the young of this season. Fat is the essential energy source needed to fuel their long periods of nocturnal flight. Researchers have determined that hummingbirds must normally develop about two grams of fat before setting out on their southward travels, compared to their entire body mass of approximately two and a half grams during the late spring when their fat content is minimal. As a result, at this time of the year, these petite-appearing creatures can be as much as 45 percent fat.

Once it has formed an appropriate deposit of fat, the hummingbird will wait until a period of favorable travel weather develops. As is the case with other birds, migration is triggered by the arrival of a Canadian high pressure system that brings with it strong northerly winds. The presence of a favorable tail wind is critical for any bird making a long distance flight.

On the day when this air mass begins to build in the area, the hummingbird will feed continuously throughout the day, much like a marathon runner loading up on carbohydrates before a big race. As evening arrives, the hummingbird, in the company of several of its neighbors, takes off on its night-long flight. Unlike a hawk, or flocks of geese, which ascend to a fairly high altitude when migrating, the hummingbird remains close to the forest canopy as it travels south.

While its eyesight is sufficient to see large obstacles at night, such as an overly tall tree that protrudes above the canopy, it is not adequate for detecting smaller objects such as high voltage electric lines or the guide wires that support communication towers. Consequently, hummingbirds, along with other migratory songsters, are known to occasionally collide with these structures. Scientists doing research on bird migration are often able to collect specimens for study by walking below a section of power line that juts above the trees.

As anyone that has tried to follow the movements of a hummingbird will surely attest, this tiny creature is one of the fastest fliers in our region. When traveling to and from a feeder, this bird has been clocked at speeds that range

from 45 to 60 mph. During long distance flights, it is believed that it seldom attains such air speeds; however, when the effects of a tail wind are added, its rate of travel probably equals or exceeds these values. This makes it possible for a small flock of hummingbirds to travel in excess of four hundred miles during the ten- to eleven-hour period of migration in which they are noted to engage. Consequently, a small flock of hummingbirds that leaves the North Country at sunset may make it to the Washington, D.C., area by sunrise the following day, if all goes well.

Hummingbirds typically rest for several weeks after such an exhausting bout of travel. During this period, they will attempt to rebuild their depleted layer of fat before heading south again on another leg of their journey. By mid-October, most of the hummingbirds from our region have arrived at the southern tip of Florida. In late October through mid-November, these birds eventually head out over the Gulf of Mexico for the coast of South America. While some birds are known to stop off in Cuba or other Caribbean islands, the majority are believed to make the entire excursion in one continuous trip.

Hummingbirds spend the winter in the equatorial regions of South America. There they feast on the nectar of the region's abundant tropical flowers in order to gradually build back a suitable layer of fat for the return trip in the spring. As the seasons change in the tropics, this tiny, iridescent bird begins its journey back to the North Country, where flowers abound, the temperatures are not too hot, and overall conditions are ideal for raising a family.

Deer Change Color

As the first few trees begin to preview the show of fall foliage that will peak in early October, another type of color transformation is occurring in the North Country. During the first few weeks of September, the white-tailed deer experiences the growth of its winter coat, which changes this animal from tannish-brown to a dark gray color.

While some mammals molt only once annually, the whitetail sheds its fur and develops a new coat of hair twice during the course of a year. In May, this regal-looking creature loses its winter coat, which is simultaneously replaced by the so-called red summer pelage. As would be expected, this coat is composed of short, relatively thin hairs that are ideal for dissipating the animal's body heat.

This chestnut-colored coat allows the deer to better blend into its summer surroundings. When light filters through a dense canopy of leaves, it diffuses to create areas of lighter shadows near the ground, especially along woodland edges where a deer spends the majority

of its time, and the reddish-brown color of its fur tends to match this summer shadowy background.

As leaves on deciduous trees turn color and drop to the ground, and grasses, weeds and fern fronds die and discolor, a pattern of sharper contrast is created. A dark gray color becomes more characteristic of the stark environment, particularly when the skies are overcast, as can happen for weeks at a time during the autumn and early winter. This change in lighting conditions prompts the change in the whitetail. (A similar, yet more drastic color change occurs in the varying hare and ermine, as an altered appearance improves the chances of being overlooked by natural enemies.)

While its deep gray color may seem appropriate for the autumn, it would appear to be quite unsuitable after the snow begins to fall. However, a dark gray coat more clearly matches the trunks of evergreen trees, especially when seen in the dim light of a dense conifer forest. Because whitetails spend so much of their time in these sheltered softwood settings in winter, their gray coat helps them blend into their surroundings despite a nearly continuous covering of snow on the ground from late November through early April.

The hair that deer begin to grow as winter approaches will eventually be much longer and thicker than the hair which covers their bodies in summer. These hairs are also slightly crinkled, rather than being totally straight. This slightly irregular shape creates a shallow fluff that establishes an insulating layer of dead air in the animal's coat. Each hair also has air chambers that further add to its insulating value. Yet, despite these features, a deer's fur is only adequate in keeping the animal warm at temperatures above -20° F. When the mercury drops below that point, this hoofed mammal is forced to move around in an attempt to generate body warmth by burning more food.

As is the case with many occurrences in nature, it is the dwindling amount of daylight that stimulates the molting process, rather than a response to the cold. An unseasonably cool August and early September will not hasten the development of a deer's winter coat, nor will a prolonged spell of hot weather at the end of the summer postpone it.

In fawns, however, the loss of the familiar spotted coat seems to be controlled by the aging process rather than light. It has been observed that only after a deer reaches the age of three months does it begin to shed its reddish-tan and white hair for its warm gray coat. In the North Country, most does give birth during the first few weeks of June, which results in the majority of fawns experiencing their color transformation around the same time as the adults. A fawn that is born late in the season will still retain its spotted pelage until it reaches twelve to fourteen weeks of age. Consequently, a fawn that is seen around Columbus Day still sporting its summer coat must have been born after the Fourth of July. This means that Bambi, who frolicked on the ice with his woodland pals while still wearing his spotted coat, would have had to be born as late as Columbus Day, which is unheard of – except in the world of Disney.

The Red-Tailed Hawk

Travel through the North Country often results in periodic sightings of a large bird of prey perched in a lone tree or within a small clump of hardwoods. Ordinarily, this very brief observation occurs where an open grassy area or brushy terrain extends a fair distance from the side of the road. This impressive creature is the red-tailed hawk, New York's most commonly-seen raptor.

The red-tail belongs to a group of diurnal birds of prey known as the buteos whose members are characterized by a robust body, rounded wing tips, and a relatively short, reddish or rusty-tan tail that fans outward when a mature bird is in flight. (It takes two full years before an individual develops the distinct plumage of a mature bird.) The milky-white underside of the red-tail is another feature that can be used to identify the hawk, and this is perhaps the easiest characteristic to note when only a glimpse of it is caught from a car window. While the osprey has a similarly colored underside, its belly plumage is a more striking white. Additionally, the osprey is almost never seen perching in a tree adjacent to a highway unless there is a sizeable body of water nearby.

The preference of the red-tail for meadowy settings arises from its inability to quickly maneuver around obstacles like tree trunks, branches, and twigs while on the attack. Open areas allow this hawk to swoop directly from its perch and make a straight line approach to whatever creature it has detected. Two other buteos that occur in the North Country, the red-shouldered hawk and the broad-winged hawk, are both far better adapted for weaving their way to the ground from a lofty perch in a more densely wooded area. As a result, both of these predators reside in forested settings where leaves, twigs, and limbs help to conceal their presence from their quarry and any human that may be passing.

From its perch well above the ground, the red-tail is able to continually scan the area below for any signs of movement. Its exceptionally keen eyesight is the result of the high density of nerve cells on its retina. This enables it to perceive details similar to those obtained by a person using binoculars. Once prey is detected, the red-tail immediately swoops to the site and attempts to grab hold of its quarry with its talons. Should it be fortunate enough to latch onto a creature with its razor sharp claws, death is virtually assured, as the puncture wounds inflicted on a small animal by the hawk's grasp are almost always fatal. Mice, voles, and rabbits are the staple items in this hawk's diet. Like most predators of this region, the red-tail will attack any suitably sized critter. Consequently, snakes, frogs, salamanders, and even large bugs like crickets and grasshoppers are snagged when the opportunity arises.

When a hawk is seen during the summer glid-ing effortlessly on rising air currents, it is not typi-cally engaged in hunt-ing. Rather, it is believed that a soaring hawk is surveying its territory for intruders. During the breeding season, hawks, particularly the red-tail, become increasingly possessive of the section of land that they have

claimed, but even after the young have fledged during the late summer and into the autumn, there is relatively little movement by the adult hawks from the area they have routinely hunted for the past months. As autumn progresses and the cold becomes more intense with each passing front of Canadian air, the journey south eventually begins. Young birds are typically the first to depart the region during October, while the adults wait until later in the season. Unlike the broad-winged hawk, which migrates in mid-September and travels in flocks that may number from several dozen to a hundred, the red-tail tends to make its way south in the company of only a few other individuals.

Locating a wintering site is more difficult for the red-tail than for other birds, as it continues to retain its territorial tendencies throughout the non-breeding season. A newly-arrived individual must be able to find a suitable hunting area that is unoccupied by other red-tails, or keep moving until it does.

During relatively mild winters, the red-tail may only venture as far south as central or southern New York. However, when colder-than-normal weather becomes entrenched over the region or a fairly deep snow pack forms, the red-tail will be forced to migrate further south. When it finds a suitable plot of open land harboring an abundance of small animals and containing several perches from which to hunt, it will take up residence until conditions improve. As the snow recedes from open areas in the North Country, the red-tail begins to reappear on those perches that overlook its breeding grounds, much to the dismay of the small creatures that reside nearby and to the delight of humans that enjoy seeing this impressive raptor.

The Monarch Butterfly Migration

It is not unusual at this time of year to note fairly large, orange and black butterflies fluttering about and sailing along, especially when the weather is more reminiscent of summer than autumn. This is the monarch butterfly, and its instinct to migrate is one of the more remarkable occurrences in nature.

162

Unlike virtually every other insect that exists in the North Country, the monarch does not simply slip into a dormant stage of its life cycle at the end of the summer and wait for favorable conditions to develop the next spring. Rather, as August progresses into September, this attractive resident of open fields and meadows begins an epic journey that takes it to the southernmost sections of the United States or into the mountains of Mexico, some two thousand miles away.

Throughout the summer, adult monarchs focus all of their attention on eating and mating. The adults that emerge from their jade blue chrysalis after Labor Day fail to expend any energy on reproducing, and concentrate all of their time feeding. While the caterpillar of this species consumes only the leaves of milkweed, the adult gets its nourishment from the nectar of flowers. At this time of the season, late blooming goldenrod, asters, and cultivated plants like mums provide much of this nectar. The increased intake of food allows for the development of a deposit of fat which helps fuel the monarch's journey.

After several days to a week of feeding, the adult monarch begins to fly south. While this butterfly is well known for remaining in open areas where flowers are abundant, it freely takes off over the large tracts of forests that cover so much of the North Country. The exact mileage covered each day varies greatly and depends entirely on the weather, since warmth is essential for maintaining a proper level of activity. According to one researcher, the monarch flies best when its body is between eighty five and one hundred degrees. While the air seldom reaches such a level at this time of the year, this butterfly is designed to increase its internal temperature by converting the sun's radiant energy into heat. The black-colored bands that extend across its wings are able to absorb most of the energy carried by the visible light portion of the spectrum, whereas the orange color is believed to be sensitive to the infra-red rays which contain a substantial portion of the sun's thermal energy. Even though the temperature of the air may be in the sixties, the monarch is able to elevate its body temperature to its optimal range whenever the sun is shining. This is why the monarch is most commonly seen at this time of the season during periods of clear, pleasant weather.

Wind is the other primary factor that impacts its rate of travel. Counterintuitively, southerly winds seem to be preferred by the Monarch for its journey southward. The warmer air carried by these winds boosts the Monarch's metabolic state and allows the butterfly to expend more energy for flight.

The ability of the monarch to know in what direction to fly, as well as which route of travel to follow, appears to be totally programmed into the genetic make-up of the insect. The individuals that make the journey in any given fall are three or four generations removed from those butterflies that arrived in the North Country during the previous May. Because the life span of an adult during the summer seldom exceeds several weeks to a month, none of the monarchs that took part in the northward journey ever live to begin a return trip.

While a monarch that reaches adulthood during the summer lives for only a short period of time, an individual that develops at the end of summer has the capability of surviving into the following spring. Although the vast majority of butterflies seen fluttering southward eventually die en route, some successfully reach their selected tropical wintering areas, where, even under favorable conditions, many more will perish, and during occasions when the weather turns downright nasty for a time, countless more will die. Yet, despite the hardships, enough always survive the winter to begin the journey back north in the spring. On the return trip, milkweed stalks in the southern states have already sprouted and are growing leaves. It is there that these few remaining butterflies lay their many eggs. Eventually, the offspring that develop into adults will complete the journey back to the North Country.

In an attempt to gain more information on the monarch's migration, numerous ecological centers across the country have been tagging and releasing these butterflies. It is hoped that enough of these marked individuals will later be observed or collected to provide researchers with better insight into some of the specifics concerning this semi-annual event.

When you are outdoors during this time of year, you should be on the lookout for large orange and black butterflies. Check to see if they are indeed heading south. If one should happen to land nearby, see if there is a small, colored tag attached to the middle section of its rear wing. If so, carefully attempt to read the information printed on it. The more data that can be collected about butterfly migration, the better able humans will be to gain an increased understanding of this remarkable event. Hopefully, we can learn enough to keep the monarch around forever.

White Pine Sheds its Needles

The pageant of leaf color that is rapidly building across the region at this time of the year involves more than just our deciduous trees. In the North Country, the white pine is a common and prominent conifer that also contributes to this display by adding a distinct shade of brown to the patchwork of color.

While the white pine retains a majority of its soft and flexible, deep green needles, this handsome conifer, along with a few closely related species, begins to shed a noticeable portion of its foliage during mid-September. The needles on the white pine live for a period of three growing seasons. This means that the bundles of needles (each containing five needles) which discolor are those that were formed on the twigs during the late spring and early summer two years previously. The needles that were formed in the current year, along with the ones that developed last season, will remain on the tree this winter.

The loss of needles on the pines at this time of year, like the shedding of broad leaves from deciduous trees, is an adaptation that allows these massive plants to better survive the winter. Although the low temperatures experienced

by this region in winter are not lethal to this or
other conifers, the exceptionally dry conditions
that are typically created by arctic air can be
devastating. The low humidity levels that accompany frigid air masses tend to draw out the
moisture that is present in many types of objects.
(It is for this reason that some people run humid-
ifiers in their homes throughout the winter.) By
shedding approximately one-third of its needles,
this conifer reduces the surface area it exposes to
the air, limiting the amount of evaporation.

The long, slender, needle-like shape of the foliage of all conifers is also an
adaptation that helps to minimize the loss of moisture to the surroundings. Since
this geometric shape has a lower amount of surface area than a broad leaf, needles are less susceptible to the drying effects of cold air. The streamlined shape
of pine needles also does not allow them to be carried very far by the wind after
they have detached from the twig. This is why it is wise to avoid parking a car
beneath a white pine during mid-September when it is shedding, as the needles
from above will land on your vehicle with little chance of them being blown off
by a midday breeze.

The needles that remain on the twigs have adapted to resist the problem of
desiccation by developing a resin that helps seal their surface. This pitch, also
present in the bark and cones, helps keep the tree as watertight as possible. The
needles of white pine also are able to clump together when conditions become
extreme. On days when the relative humidity is low or when there is a wind, the
white pine's needles move directly alongside adjacent needles to create tighter
than normal clusters. In this way, the surface area exposed to the wind is reduced even further. During periods of such inclement weather, the concentrated
bundles of needles give the branches of the white pine a distinctively thin or
emaciated appearance. In contrast, during periods of warm and sunny weather in
early to mid-autumn, when the tree can still engage in photosynthesis, the needles
separate as much as possible in order to capture a maximum amount of sunlight.
On these pleasant September and October days, the twigs take on a much more
feathery, fuller appearance.

As colder weather becomes the rule, the food manufacturing process in this and other evergreens gradually ceases due to the lack of water, an essential ingredient for photosynthesis. As the ground freezes, all plants lose the ability to absorb moisture through their roots. Moisture levels in the woody conducting tissues also drop as a way for a tree to survive winter's below-freezing temperatures. This lowers the point at which the water molecules will freeze to a temperature that is unlikely to occur in our region. Even though the temperature may periodically rise above thirty two degrees during mild periods in mid-winter, photosynthesis will not occur until the ground begins to thaw.

As soon as water can again be absorbed in the spring, the process of food production quickly commences, since these trees already have their needles in place. As is the case with other conifers and with deciduous trees, new greenery does not emerge from its buds until well into the spring. The needles that emerge on the twigs of the white pine will remain in place for three full summers, after which they will also turn rusty-brown in color and fall to the forest floor, adding a fresh layer of dead matter to the soil below.

Spider Webs

Few objects in nature are made more visible when highlighted by morning sunlight and the heavy dew of the late summer and early autumn than spider webs. While these delicate silken structures are nearly transparent from midday throughout the afternoon, they develop an attractive translucence when condensation coats them with tiny beads of water.

Since objects in open areas collect the greatest amounts of dew, webs that are located in gardens, fields, brushy areas, and on lawns are the ones most likely to be seen. Ordinarily, only one particular type of web seems to be present in any localized setting. Even though many species of spiders may reside there, conditions often temporarily favor one species over the others in that immediate area. A single pair of adults is capable of producing hundreds of offspring that can grow rapidly when weather and food conditions are particularly favorable to their species. Should there be a lack of natural enemies at that site, a localized population can quickly swell, and a vast number of webs of a single design can suddenly appear.

While the intricate design of a spider web gives the impression that this structure requires a few days of toil to complete, these highly effective bug snares take only a few hours to construct. Consequently, dozens of webs may pop up overnight or during the course of a few days in a spot where a particular species has become locally abundant.

The rapid rate at which a spider can construct a web often proves to be frustrating to people with a dislike for these structures, particularly those located close to a door or across a walkway. A person may completely knock down one or several webs in the morning, only to find more in similar or identical locations the following day. If you wish to eliminate spider webs around your home, it is necessary to capture those individuals responsible for these structures and remove them from the area. A spider typically lurks just above its web during the daytime and may occasionally be spotted on it. This allows the spider to quickly attack a bug that happens to come into contact with the web before the victim can free itself from the silken trap.

Of the three basic spider web designs, the orb shape is the one that generally comes to mind. These circular webs tend to be erected vertically, in order to net insects that fly horizontally, and they are often placed between sticks, twigs, and other objects that serve as likely avenues for traveling bugs. They are also frequently located under the eaves of houses, especially near a porch light which attracts insects flying at night.

The threads of the orb web are composed of two different types of silk. First, there is a framework of supporting fibers and strands that radiate from a central hub. The silk used in making these elements is smooth and sturdy. The cross fibers that connect these rays together and give the orb web its mesh-like characteristic are known as viscid spiral threads. A close examination of these cross threads with a powerful magnifying glass, especially on a dry afternoon, should reveal their rough or lumpy surface texture. These irregularities are the result of a secretion that is placed on the silk to increase its sticky quality.

When an orb web spider has been eating well and is in a good state of health, it usually cuts away and discards these viscid spiral threads every night and replaces them with fresh ones. This is done to ensure its net will maintain as high an adhesive quality as possible.

Another group of webs is produced by the funnel-web weavers. These spiders spin relatively dense, horizontal or flat webs that slope into a hole located somewhat off center. Upon encountering this pitched platform, a bug follows its contour toward the neck of the funnel, where it is ambushed by the web maker. After killing its victim, the spider retreats to the neck of the funnel, where it will consume the remains and then wait for another victim.

The design of the last category of spider webs is characterized by its lack of consistency, rather than by its symmetry. Simply referred to as cobwebs, these highly irregular silken structures (well known for their dust-collecting ability) are the handiwork of comb-footed spiders. Like an orb or funnel web, the dense

crisscrossing fibers produced by the comb-footed spiders are produced solely for capturing bugs.

In the North Country there are various other spiders that never build a web. These arachnids rely on stalking skills and speed to capture their prey. Their silk-spinning ability is reserved for locomotion, especially during the early autumn when many young individuals are dispersing. Since they do not have webs that become covered with dew, the presence of these spiders is difficult to detect unless you happen to walk face first into one of the long threads they use to carry themselves to new and different places.

The Harvestmen

With its eight, lengthy, thread-like legs, the daddy-longlegs bears a superficial resemblance to spiders. However, these arachnids, also known as harvestmen, have structural features and behavioral traits which cause them to be classified into a category of their own.

In appearance, a daddy-longlegs is characterized by an oval-shaped body that does not seem to be divided into two distinct sections, as a spider's is. While a similar form of segmentation does exist within its body, this structure is not at all apparent when looking at this familiar, grayish-brown backyard bug.

Silk glands are absent from the harvestmen, and this affects the manner in which they acquire food and move from place to place. Rather than wait for insects to become ensnared in their webs, these part-time predators prowl an area for small organisms to kill. Because they lack both fangs and a venom sac, daddy-longlegs are unable to subdue the larger bugs which spiders routinely attack, and they pose no threat to the well-being of humans, as they cannot bite or inject any toxic substance, as spiders do. In order to find enough to eat, the daddy-longlegs are known to scavenge dead animal matter. Even the remains of selected plants may be used as a food source by these arachnids.

The daddy-longlegs locates food as it moves, for the tips of its spindly legs, especially the second set from the front, contain various sense organs that pick up

the smell emitted by aphids, mites, and other arthropods of similar size. Harvest-men are also able to sense the minute vibrations produced by young grubs and other soil-dwelling larvae as they move just below the surface. In a similar man-ner, these arachnids are able to detect the presence of tiny wood-dwelling organ-isms that live directly beneath the bark of trees.

While the daddy-longlegs has a set of eyes on the top of its head, these organs are used solely for detecting the presence of natural enemies and not to locate food. Birds, shrews, toads, large predatory insects, and spiders are all known to attack these gangly arachnids. If grabbed by one of its legs, the ap-pendage will immediately detach and begin to twitch rapidly. This violent movement is designed to distract the attacker for a second or two, providing the victim with a brief opportunity to escape. If it is successful in avoiding capture, a harvestman will not regenerate a new appendage to replace the one that was lost; it simply goes through the rest of the season with one less leg. This is why a daddy-longlegs may be seen with only seven or sometimes six legs, particularly as summer wanes.

As asters come into bloom and apples become ready to harvest, daddy-longlegs reach the adult stage of their life cycle and begin to breed. After mat-ing, females seek out an appropriate place in which to deposit their eggs. Even though these arachnids commonly reside in open places, such as flower beds, vegetable gardens, and agricultural fields, spots that are sheltered from the rain and snow are normally favored by females looking to lay eggs. The nooks and crannies around the foundation of a house, the back corner of a wood shed, or the space beneath an overturned canoe may all serve as an overwintering site for the eggs. Even though these arachnids commonly reside around houses, they, unlike several other species of spiders, seldom stray indoors.

It may seem that the overall impact the harvestmen have on the ecology of the North Country is minimal at best. Although they do not have as profound an effect in controlling the population of smaller bugs as do many other creatures, the contributions made by these benign arachnids to the intricate web of life are still vital. All living things, regardless of their role in nature, are essential to the overall health and well being of an environment. These delicate organisms add a special dimension to the world that exists beneath our feet and which remains, all too often, hidden from our sight.

The Cedar Waxwing

There are numerous birds that take advantage of the abundance of berries that exist in the North Country throughout the summer and into the autumn. Among those that reap this harvest of wild fruits is a colorful and regal-looking bird known as the cedar waxwing.

From the late spring through mid-autumn, this handsome brown bird with the crested head may be seen anyplace where juicy, covered seeds abound. During June, the tiny strawberries which grow in fields and lawns and along roadsides are a main component of the waxwing's early season diet. So, too, are the plain red fruits of shadbush and serviceberry that grow on the edges of many of our rivers, streams, and lakes.

During the early to mid-summer, when cedar waxwings have a nest full of young to feed, adults turn their attention to capturing bugs. As a result, these attractive birds may be seen plucking an insect from the air, as would a flycatcher, or picking a caterpillar, beetle, or spider from the surface of a leaf or twig, as warblers do. Because rapidly-growing babies require a diet rich in protein rather than carbohydrates, their parents must temporarily target invertebrates for their source of food. By the time the young fledge, their need for animal matter decreases, and berries gradually become the staple in their diet.

As the weeks pass and different crops ripen (and some fail to properly do so), the cedar waxwing will shift its foraging location to any area in which it can find an adequate supply of fruits. Since the weather dictates the type of growing season that an area experiences, the quality of a crop of wild fruits can vary greatly from one year to the next, which likewise impacts the presence of cedar waxwings.

While midsummer provides the cedar waxwing with a variety of berries, September is often the peak of our wild fruit season and the period with the richest supply of food for this bird. In the weeks following Labor Day, before our area experiences autumn's first hard frost, there are still blackberries on their thorny canes and ripened wild black cherries and choke cherries dangling from their

twigs. Wild raisins, nannyberries, the fruits of honeysuckle, and an assortment of other wild edibles that are too numerous to list are also available after school has started for the year. Since semi-open settings provide the best conditions for the growth of many of these plants, it is generally in forest clearings, woodland borders, and shrub-laden areas that small flocks of cedar waxwings are most frequently seen and heard.

While the vast majority of North Country birds gather together in flocks as the summer draws to a close, the cedar waxwing is well known for its gregarious behavior throughout the entire year. Unlike nearly every other bird, this creature never hesitates to temporarily leave its small nesting territory, even during the height of its breeding season, in order to accompany other cedar waxwings in the search for food. After foraging with the group for an hour or so, each bird eventually returns to its nest to continue its parental chores.

Because individuals frequently lose sight of one another as they hop behind leaves and through dense clumps of vegetation in their quest for berries, these song birds attempt to remain in vocal contact with the flock by periodically uttering a high-pitched note. This is the characteristic "tseee" call, a short, monotone hissing-whistle that keeps the birds aware of each-other's whereabouts. It is also frequently given in flight as an invitation to other cedar waxwings below to join the foraging flock.

When colder weather comes to the region, the cedar waxwing remains in the area as long as some fruit remains on small trees, shrubs, and vines. Although some of these remaining wild berries are not suitable for human consumption, most can be eaten by the cedar waxwing – our region's number one berry picker. As fresh fruit becomes less available, these birds are forced to stray further in their daily search for food, eventually beginning to work their way south. While some cedar waxwings are known to travel as far south as Central America, others remain in our southern and central states, feeding on dried berries, fallen seeds, and an occasional bug or two while they await the return of spring and berry-picking time in the North Country.

October

The Timber Rattlesnake

Old stone walls, rock ledges, and boulder-strewn hillsides are all common haunts of the eastern timber rattlesnake, yet this venomous reptile will never be encountered in these settings throughout most of the North Country, as conditions are quite unsuitable for this maligned creature in the vast majority of our region.

Because of its cold-blooded physiology, the timber rattlesnake, like nearly all reptiles, strongly prefers places with a milder, more temperate climate than that which is common throughout most of our region. In fact, when examining the geographic distribution of this snake, it can be noted that selected locations near Lake George and in the lowlands around Lake Champlain form the very northern edge of its range. Since both of these areas possess a climate that is more like central sections of New York State than like the Adirondacks, this reptile is able to eke out an existence in favorable rocky habitats in these specific locations. However, in ever slightly higher elevations close by, conditions quickly become unacceptable for this northern species of rattlesnake. And while the St. Lawrence River Valley and the northern portion of the Lake Ontario Basin have weather conditions that resemble those within the Champlain Valley, several factors conspire to exclude this snake from these areas.

Along with a tolerable climate and a favorable habitat on geologically-acceptable terrain, suitable hibernating sites must also exist if the timber rattlesnake is to successfully reside in a given location. Such sites typically occur on south-facing slopes, in deep crevices or fissures in rock outcrops that allow this rather robust snake to get far enough below ground to reach areas where the temperature will remain above freezing throughout the winter, regardless of how cold the air becomes. There also has to be a chamber or cavern large enough to accommodate the many dozens to occasionally a hundred or more snakes that cluster together in these winter dens. The eastern timber rattlesnake may migrate from one to two and a-half miles during early to mid-autumn to get to a suitable hibernating site in which to spend the winter.

Around such sites, great concentrations of timber rattlesnakes can be found prior to and immediately following their period of hibernation. Humans bent on exterminating this snake are often able to destroy major portions of a population by focusing their attention during the fall, and again in the spring, on areas around a winter den. While the timber rattlesnake was never common in the Champlain and Upper Hudson River Valley, their numbers have declined greatly

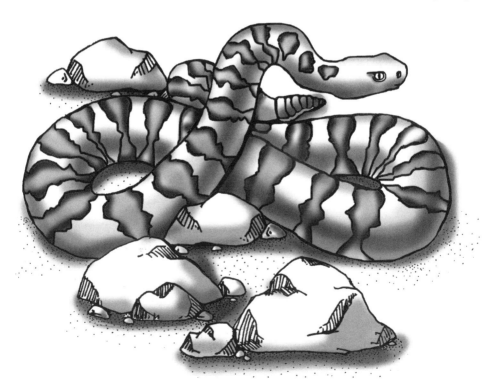

over the past century because of such hunting practices.

An effort to reverse this trend in New York has been made by placing this ecologically beneficial reptile on the State's list of threatened species. However, it will take many decades, if not centuries, before the danger of its elimination from the far northern fringe of its range is assured. Unlike most forms of wildlife, the rattlesnake has an exceptionally low rate of reproduction. It is estimated by researchers that a baby rattler requires from eight to ten years to reach sexual maturity. Additionally, an adult female may give birth to only a half dozen or so young every three years. Consequently, it takes scores of years for rattlesnakes to repopulate an area decimated by snake hunters.

Like the wolf, the timber rattlesnake has experienced some very bad publicity over the years in both literature and in films. Contrary to popular belief, this reptile is exceptionally wary of humans and is considered to be non-aggressive. Rather than confront an intruder, it will either hide or quickly retreat from the immediate area. It is not uncommon for this rattlesnake to slither into a rock cubby in order to avoid being seen by a passerby. As long as a person does not reach into its hiding place in an effort to grab it, the odds that he or she will be attacked are slim to none. In fact, the chance of being bitten by an eastern timber rattlesnake while hiking in the North Country is comparable to that of being hit by a meteor.

The Last Days of the Woodchuck

Around the time when deciduous trees start to shed their leaves en masse in preparation for the coming winter, the woodchuck (also known as the groundhog) responds to the change in seasons by retreating into its burrow and slipping into a state of hibernation. Although periods of pleasant weather can still occur for another month, the woodchuck typically begins its very lengthy state of dormancy when the growing season comes to an end.

Like cows and horses, the woodchuck is an animal that depends heavily on grasses, clover, weeds, and various types of cultivated plants, especially those found in the garden, for its food. However, unlike domestic livestock, the woodchuck does not fancy hay or other types of dead plant matter that have been thoroughly dried. As a rule, the more lush or succulent the vegetation, the more attractive it is to this rather large, ground-dwelling rodent. Consequently, as goldenrod, asters, and other late summer plants die and turn brown following the first hard frost, the woodchuck finds itself in an environment that is devoid of anything to eat.

Because of its dependency on non-woody vegetation, the woodchuck frequents open fields and meadows where such plants abound. However, this member of the squirrel family also likes the cover afforded by scattered clumps of trees and shrubby thickets, especially to conceal the entrance to its underground burrow. As a result, the woodchuck generally prefers to inhabit forest edges like the grassy slopes of ski hills, the infrequently mowed areas around golf course fairways, and the strip of land that runs along the side of major roads and highways that cut through forested areas.

During the summer, a woodchuck may opt to maintain a burrow complex in a completely open area where there are few if any trees around, but as the late

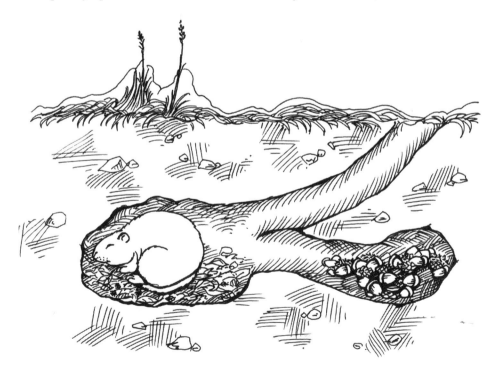

summer progresses into early autumn, and the time for hibernation nears, these individuals usually relocate to settings in which a wooded border is present. There, it seeks out a spot for its den where there is a definite pitch to the terrain. By placing the entrance to its subterranean home on a well-drained hillside, the woodchuck reduces the chances of having water seep into its nest during rainy periods. A sizeable mound of soil arcing around the lower portion of the main entrance makes the presence of a woodchuck's burrow quite conspicuous. However, this creature also constructs a secondary entrance that does not have any soil around it and which is typically placed under the base of a tree or alongside a boulder. It is from this secretive opening that the woodchuck peers outward to check for intruders before it exits the safety of its burrow.

Throughout the summer, the woodchuck grazes heavily on the tenderest nutrient-enriched plants that grow in open areas. In the process of ingesting massive quantities of vegetation, the woodchuck develops a substantial layer of fat that often equals or exceeds 40 percent of its springtime weight. It is this deposit of fat that fuels its body processes over the course of the next six to seven months while the woodchuck remains dormant in its underground nest.

Unlike the bear and raccoon, which merely sleep through the winter, the woodchuck experiences a very profound state of unconsciousness when it hibernates. Its heartbeat is known to drop from an average of one hundred beats per minute to a level of only a half dozen or so beats per minute. Its rate of respiration also diminishes substantially, as does its body temperature, which can fall into the mid-forties. In this way, the internal food reserves of the woodchuck are depleted at a slow enough rate to last until that time in the spring when the shoots of emerging plants begin to sprout.

During the summer, it is fairly common to see this rather portly brown critter sitting off the shoulder of a road nibbling on the grass that a highway crew was unable to reach with a mower. But by October, the cellular structure of the grass and surrounding weeds has become too tough and indigestible for the woodchuck. It will not be until the sun's warmth stimulates new growth in the thawing soil the following spring that this burrowing critter will again grace the edges of our highways and fairways, or, much to the owner's chagrin, a healthy garden or farm field.

Woodcock Migration

Among the many animals in the North Country that feed on earthworms is an odd-looking bird known as the woodcock. Rather than being nocturnal or diurnal, this plump bird with stubby legs and an exceptionally long bill maintains an unusual feeding schedule. It is mostly crepuscular, which means that it searches for its food during the twilight periods of dawn and dusk.

Shortly after the sun sets, the woodcock leaves its daytime retreat to search for worms by inserting its long, slender bill into the soft and relatively rich soil of damp woods and alder thickets. Since its bill contains highly specialized nerve tissue that can sense the vibrations produced by bugs as they move through the dirt, the woodcock is able to locate their position by using it to probe the soil. After detecting a potential meal, the woodcock then pushes its bill into the exact spot that harbors its prey, and the special hook-tip enables this bird to hang on to any squirmy invertebrate caught as it is being extracted from the soil. While it eats most bugs as soon as they are encountered, the woodcock has a special preference for worms, and it will pass over other critters if it has an opportunity to snag a night crawler.

The woodcock typically probes the soil for up to an hour during the evening twilight until it becomes too dark for it to see. On extremely bright nights when the moon is near full, it has been reported to feed for longer periods, but it generally remains inactive throughout the night until the eastern sky begins to brighten ever so slightly. At that time it engages in another round of foraging, until it has either satisfied its appetite or has become nervous about being seen by a predator as daylight begins to make its presence increasingly more conspicuous.

With its mottled tan, brown, gray, and white plumage, the woodcock is colored and shaded exactly like the ground, especially in alder thickets and in certain types of hardwood forests. So effective is its camouflage as it sits against a backdrop of dead alder, aspen, cherry, and birch leaves that it often goes unnoticed by our many woodland predators. Consequently, the woodcock is most reluctant to move during times of bright light, as it instinctively knows that its best defense is to simply sit quietly among the leaf litter and wait for the shadowy period of twilight to occur.

Occasionally, the whistling-twitter sound produced when a woodcock takes to the air may be heard as daylight fades in the very late afternoon. Because of the shape of the ends of its three leading primary flight feathers, the woodcock's wings create a unique sound during an accelerated period of upward flight. When it takes off from a daytime resting spot to visit a twilight feeding location, this bird's presence can be easily noted, even though dim light conditions may prevent a good view of the bird.

During the spring, when worms are readily available in open, grassy settings, the woodcock may be regularly seen and heard after sunset around large lawns and fields. However, as the soil heats up and dries out during the summer, worms push their way further down, beyond the reach of the woodcock. Consequently, this bird then limits its foraging activities to places where the soil remains moist and worms are more likely to remain within its grasp.

As the intensity of the sun decreases following the equinox and rainier weather becomes more common, conditions of the soil become more favorable for bugs and worms in open areas. This allows the woodcock to expand its feeding range, which is important for building the layer of fat that it needs to fuel its

migration south. Soon, with the onset of colder weather, most invertebrates lapse into a dormant period, which makes their detection nearly impossible. Additionally, as the soil begins to freeze, the woodcock loses the ability to insert its bill into the ground to explore for food.

In the North Country, the woodcock's southward migration normally occurs toward the end of October. At this time, small flocks of these birds may be seen or heard during the late evening as they take off from an alder thicket. Inevitably, there are a few individuals that remain well into November; these are birds that have come across a spot in which the ground has failed to succumb to the first few hard frosts and still contains an abundant and active population of earthworms.

Cranberry Season

Despite the fact that the growing season has ended in many locations throughout the North Country, there is still one crop of wild edibles that is just now ripening. It is not until the leaves begin to fall en masse and the first hard frost has killed many temperature-sensitive plants that cranberries become ready to harvest.

Cranberries are a small group of low, creeping, miniature, vine-like plants that are closely related to blueberries. However, unlike their sweet-tasting relatives, which grow in the dry soil of open areas, cranberries thrive in the harsh chemical world of bogs. In the cranberries' attempt to survive in these water-logged, acid-laden meadows, they have evolved several features that result in their exceptionally late fruit formation.

In a bog there is virtually no current or exchange of fresh water. As the water sits undisturbed for long periods of time, most, if not all, of the dissolved oxygen becomes exhausted. Even microorganisms such as bacteria of decay that need only trace amounts of this life-sustaining gas begin to suffer, and they eventually become unable to continue with their process of breaking down the organic matter that has fallen into the water. This creates deposits of once-living debris that is only partially rotted, a situation that results in an abundance of humic acid in the surroundings. (It is this acid that contaminates bog water and stains it a characteristic brown or chocolate color.)

Since most of the dead matter that accumulates in bogs never gets completely broken down into the simple molecules that plants need to absorb, a nutrient-deficient environment is formed. Cranberries, like most other bog plants, have adapted, in part, by becoming evergreen rather than being deciduous. This allows these plants to channel the very limited amount of nutrients that are taken from the soil into growth and fruit production, rather than leaf formation.

Since the leaves of the cranberries are always present, these plants are capable of starting photosynthesis much earlier in the spring and continuing well into the autumn. Consequently, the berries remain attached to the stems in an attempt to collect carbohydrates manufactured late in the season.

The deep red color of the cranberries is also believed to help these plants continue to remain actively engaged in photosynthesis as the weather cools, as it is ideal for absorbing the sun's infrared rays and converting them into heat, thereby elevating the temperature of the plant. Also, since cranberries grow in and around aquatic areas, the fog that typically occurs on frosty nights during this season helps protect them against freezing temperatures.

Because they grow in such harsh chemical conditions, cranberries have developed some of the same properties that retard the action of the bacteria of decay. This is why these popular autumn berries may be kept after being harvested for longer periods of time than other fruits without experiencing spoilage. Additionally, medical researchers tell us that cranberries contain substances absorbed from their acid environment that limit the action of bacteria in the urinary tract of humans. This is why cranberry juice is recommended for treating mild cases of bladder infection.

While bogs and the other wet sites that harbor cranberries commonly occur in the North Country, finding a place where these fruits are plentiful is not easy. As is the case with many fruit-producing plants, only scattered berries form on its tiny twigs, and growing conditions are rarely good enough to allow for a bumper crop of these berries. Additionally, creatures such as raccoons, bears, and various rodents will consume them whenever they get the chance. A site which yields an abundance of cranberries is a valuable asset to an individual who enjoys these tart treats. This is why it is so important to keep good cranberry patches a secret, especially from so-called friends that likewise may have a fond taste for these late autumn berries.

Beechnuts

Although berries, nuts, and seeds serve as a source of food to one population of animals or another, the quality and quantity of nutrients present in these structures are not all equal. While some fruits, such as cranberries, contain a limited reserve of food and are eaten by only certain bog-frequenting creatures, beechnuts contain a high concentration of nutrients and are sought by most forms of wildlife.

A beechnut is composed of a tasty kernel of matter covered by a tough skin or inner shuck on three sides, giving it a unique triangular shape. A pair of these nuts is encased in a rounded, spiny-covered outer casing that develops on the twig of the beech tree. As the nuts mature, and as cool, dry mid-autumn air settles over the region, the outer shuck begins to split and eventually curves backward, exposing the nuts. Occasionally, gravity alone is sufficient to pull these small brown masses from their opened casings. However, their attachment at the top is often strong enough to hold them in place until they are knocked loose when shaken by a strong wind. The rattling of the branches during a stiff breeze can also break dried and partially open shucks free. Yet, even during years when early autumn gales frequently buffet the region, only a few ripened nuts ever appear on the ground prior to the Columbus Day weekend, as the bulk of this crop normally falls later in the month.

Occasionally, numerous shucks may be found beneath a few select beech trees before the leaves fall. These probably have not dropped of their own accord but have been cut by a squirrel. Because of the extreme competition for these highly nutritious and meaty nuts, squirrels are known for their determined efforts to harvest a portion of this crop before they ripen. Rather than gather them from some precarious perch at the end of a twig, red, gray, and flying squirrels, along with chipmunks, simply sever the unopened shucks from the limbs and let them drop to the ground. After spending ten to fifteen minutes working in a section of the crown of the tree, the animal will descend to the ground to collect as many of the fallen nuts as it can find.

The black bear is another creature that will ascend a healthy beech tree in order to collect the nuts before they fall. Once it has reached a place in the crown where it can sit, such as a crotch in the trunk, the bear will reach out and pull in the smaller limbs that contain the nuts, sometimes breaking them in order to ac-

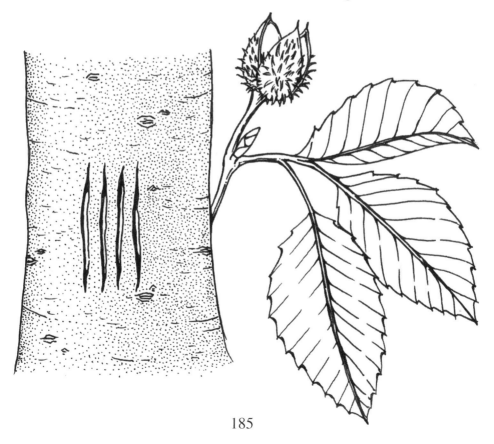

185

cess those nuts near the very end. Elongated gashes in the smooth gray bark of a beech trunk serve as a record that a bear was there. (The largest claw marks are those created when the bear descends the trunk, rather than goes up it.) A sizeable collection of broken branches in a crotch is another indication that a bear has foraged for nuts above the forest floor.

During good years, a small rodent may be able to gather enough beechnuts to last it for an entire year. In the North Country, most chipmunks will not enter into their state of winter dormancy until the last of the beechnuts has been gleaned from the forest floor around their burrow. In some cases, these striped rodents will remain active, collecting fallen beechnuts despite a covering of snow on the ground. Hibernation begins only when the individuals can no longer find a sufficient number of beechnuts to make it worth their while.

The relative abundance of beechnuts produced each year varies more than that of any other crop of wild edibles. There are many autumns when beech trees fail to yield any of these tasty morsels of food. Following such nut-less seasons, many of the animals that depend on them for building a cache of food and putting on a layer of fat to carry them through to the spring encounter fatal hardships.

Even during years when many seemingly ripened nuts appear on a beech tree, it is possible that a high percentage of these have been attacked by nut-eating invertebrates and decomposing microbes. Several types of bugs and selected strains of fungi can seriously impact the formation of beechnuts as they develop during the summer. Consequently, it is not uncommon to find nuts on the ground and discover, when the brown exterior husk has been peeled back, that they do not contain any kernel of concentrated food.

The list of creatures that consume beechnuts is lengthy, as even many predatory animals such as foxes and coyotes will feast on these nuts. This is the primary reason why, despite their abundance on the ends of upper twigs and branches during years when growing conditions are favorable, only a few scattered beechnuts are available for those humans who enjoy nibbling on these small, natural treats.

Tamarack Sheds its Needles

During the final weeks of October, scattered patches of yellow forest can be seen amidst the gray background of bare branches and stark trunks. While nearly all of our deciduous trees have changed color and dropped their leaves, two holdouts are only now losing their chlorophyll and displaying their amber leaf pigments.

The final splash of gold in low-lying areas where water collects and saturates the soil is caused by the American larch, better known as the tamarack. The wooded rims of bogs, the edges of conifer swamps, and drainage areas on the sides of highways are all settings in which the light brownish-yellow color of the tamarack is likely to appear. Tamarack may also infrequently create a thin canopy in drier sites where the soil is acidic and trees are widely scattered. In these semi-open settings, the tamarack occasionally grows alongside the quaking aspen, the other tree of the North Country that changes color very late in the season.

Aside from its late color transformation, the tamarack is unique among deciduous trees because it is a conifer. Rather than developing its seeds in the same structural way as do broad-leafed trees, the tamarack forms them inside a cone,

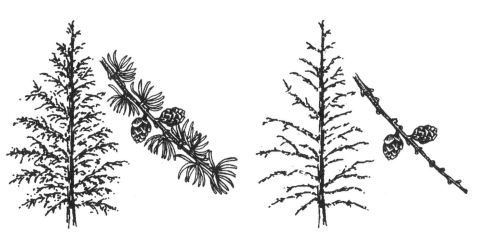

187

much like pines, spruces, and firs. And like other conifers, this tree possesses needle-like foliage as opposed to wide, papery leaves.

Tamarack needles are about an inch in length and are arranged in a circular cluster that contains in excess of fifteen needles. On the very end of its thin twigs, however, the tamarack's needles often appear singularly, rather than in distinct radial clumps.

While a tamarack's needles may look like those of other conifers, their texture is quite different. Because the tamarack sheds its needles each autumn, the needles do not have to be sealed against the loss of internal moisture to the dry winter air, as do the needles of an evergreen. As a result, rather than being covered by wax and filled with a resin that produces a stiffness to these long structures, the needles of the tamarack possess a remarkably soft and delicate quality that makes them pleasurable to the touch.

By undergoing this autumn process of shedding its needles, the tamarack, like other deciduous trees, is attempting to protect itself from the desiccating effects that winter air has on plants. In fact, this ability to withstand the potentially lethal dehydrating effects that arctic weather has on green forms of life is better developed in the tamarack than in nearly any other species of tree on this continent, enabling it to flourish as far north as any tree in North America.

In its attempt to generate enough stored nutrients to allow for the formation of new needles in the spring, the tamarack extends its period of photosynthesis longer into the autumn than any other deciduous tree. However, by this time in the season, cold blasts of dry arctic air can be expected to push into the northeast, thereby creating conditions that are unfavorable for retaining soft, unprotected foliage. This is why even the tamarack succumbs to the inevitable change in seasons and sheds its needles.

Among the tamarack's adaptations for surviving in wet areas is the ability of its trunk and branches to resist rotting when exposed to constant moisture. This durability, along with the wood's hardness and relative strength, makes it ideal for use in places that are often damp. Before the age of creosote treatment or pressure-treated processes, tamarack was the preferred wood for use as telephone poles, railroad ties, and dock pilings.

The sight of a stand of softwood trees with all of their needles turning a dull yellowish-brown and dropping to the ground ordinarily indicates an area of timber in a poor state of health. However, if these conifers exist near a body of water or sit in a lowland setting, chances are that they are a cluster of tamaracks preparing for winter.

A Deer's Sense of Smell

Of a deer's three main senses, the ability to detect and discern odors is believed to provide the whitetail with the greatest amount of information about its surroundings, especially when it is in densely wooded areas or in fields covered with tall grasses, weeds, and shrubs that can severely limit its availability to see. Additionally, a carpet of needles or moist leaves on the ground can prevent the padded paws of a predator like a coyote or bobcat from easily being heard. Although both its eyesight and hearing are extremely acute and of vital importance to its survival, a deer's sense of smell is more useful in finding food, avoiding danger, and locating the other deer that reside in that same general area.

It has been estimated that a whitetail's nose is some four hundred times more sensitive to odors than that of a human. (This approximation is based on an analysis of the density and overall extent of the nerve endings in its olfactory system.) This enables a deer to detect even minute concentrations of scent molecules emitted by food and other animals in the environment. For example, over-ripened apples, cherries, and raspberries that have fallen to the ground all produce their own characteristic odors. Since smells can travel for a considerable distance and can permeate through the forest cover, a deer's nose can alert it to such sources of food and any potential dangers that may be out of view. While a deer eventually learns where food can be obtained during the different seasons, it is its sense of smell that initially leads it to the exact spots.

As it walks, the whitetail emits its own trace amounts of scent from glands located between the two hooves on its feet. This creates a scent trail that any other deer can follow, often for up to a day after it was made. As a deer bounds, more of this scent is dislodged from these glands, creating an area of higher scent density. As a result, a deer's scent trail not only indicates the route which a deer has traveled but also any places where it was startled and forced to run. If a deer suspects danger, it will stomp its front feet on the ground in order to place more scent at that site. This marks that spot and alerts other deer to the potential for danger there.

As breeding or rutting season approaches over the next several weeks, deer begin to constantly communicate their reproductive status to one another by means of scent. As a doe nears her estrus or heat period, she releases special chemicals called pheromones into her urine. When a buck detects urine containing this stimulating fragrance, it will immediately follow the female's scent trail until he eventually overtakes her. This is why a buck may occasionally be seen traveling through an area with its nose toward the ground, rather than with its head held in the more typical upward position that provides it with a better field of vision. After finding a doe and breeding with her, a buck will remain with her for several days to prevent a rival buck from mating with her. In this way, the male ensures that the fawns produced from its reproductive encounter will

contain his genetic information.

A buck also creates scent posts at this time of the year. This notifies the does that there is a male in the area and that their breeding needs will eventually be satisfied. A buck's scent post serves as a warning to other males in the area that a physical confrontation will result if they are detected around does in the vicinity that are nearing their heat period.

As is the case with any creature that depends heavily on a sense of smell, a deer will attempt to keep its nose as moist as possible in order to more effectively detect odors. This is because scent molecules react better with nerve cells in the nose if they are accompanied by water. Consequently, as the moisture level of the air inhaled through the nasal passages increases, the ability to sense fragrances also is enhanced. As a means of getting as accurate an assessment of a scent as possible, a deer often forcefully expels air through its nasal passage. This helps to moisten the nasal membrane and eliminates any distracting scents that may happen to be present. This reflex reaction results in a unique whistling noise that can be heard a hundred yards away.

Over the course of the next month and a half, hunters will be attempting to locate the big bucks that roam our fields and forests. While this is indeed a challenge for a human, it is not so difficult for a deer, as these creatures have a snout that is able to detect the presence of this threat.

A Deer's Sense of Sight

An exceptionally keen sense of sight is essential for maneuvering through a dimly lit and densely wooded area. While smells provide a whitetail with information about the location of food and other deer, eyesight is the sense it employs to avoid the inanimate objects all around it, assess the nature of the terrain, and detect danger that may be lurking in areas that are downwind.

Like nocturnal animals, a deer has enlarged sight organs that are adapted for gathering an increased amount of radiant energy. Additionally, these structures have an internal reflective quality that causes light to bounce around inside, which aids in its amplification. In this way, a deer is able to travel through a wooded glade and avoid the many obstacles in its path, even well after the sun has set.

Studies done on the retina of a deer indicate that this light-sensitive tissue at the back of the eye possesses an especially high concentration of rod cells. Rods are the nerves that are responsive to any form of visible light; they provide an animal with a detailed black-and-white image of its surroundings. In general, the relative density of rod cells in the retina determines the creature's ability to decipher outline, detect motion, and see under dim light conditions. Since a deer's vision is primarily based on rod cells, this big-eyed animal is able to see well at night and can quickly pick out any moving object. This is why it is important for a hunter on watch to remain as still as possible, as any movement is easily detected by the rod cells of the whitetail.

Human eyes have a fair number of rod cells; however, these miraculous structures are mostly concentrated along the sides of our retina rather than at the

back. This is why motion coming from an object that is off-center is more likely to catch our attention and why peripheral vision, rather than straight-ahead sight, becomes more effective for seeing at night.

Cone cells are the nerve cells activated by specific frequencies of visible light, thereby providing information about color. The more cone cells contained in the retina, the better an animal's ability to perceive color. While deer do have some cone cells, these receptors, like those that occur in a human's eye, cease to function during conditions of minimal illumination. As a result, a low level of light reflected off a red-checkered hunting coat may not be adequate to activate the cone cells that are sensitive to these colors. Since minimally intense rays are adequate to stimulate rod cells, the coat and hunter will be visible to a deer; however, both will appear in a black-and-white form and may not be interpreted as anything of concern.

Because deer are most active during the early morning and late afternoon, a time when light intensity is low, especially in densely wooded settings, these creatures are effectively color blind at these times. This is also the case during periods of heavy overcast, particularly in stands of conifers.

During the middle of the day or whenever the sun is out, however, a whitetail is believed to be able to see the red or orange worn by many safety-conscious individuals as they venture into the woods. Whether the sight of these bright colors triggers any alarm in a deer is a point of debate. Some sportsmen claim that while deer can see this red color, they generally do not associate it with danger. In fact, some hunters maintain that a red or orange coat is not viewed any differently than a clump of red or orange leaves. Others contend that a person in bright clothing standing against a darker background would create a silhouette that the rod cells would easily detect. Since camouflage helps to break up this type of outline, its use during this time of the day is deemed essential by many big-game enthusiasts.

Clothing that has bright red and orange patches meshed into an irregular camouflage pattern is considered to be an excellent choice for people who wish to stand out to other humans, while remaining relatively unnoticeable to deer. Regardless of the type of attire that you feel should be worn during deer season, it is universally agreed that a dark brown jacket with a piece of white cloth hanging from the back edge should never be worn, especially by an individual who has a bounding gait to his style of movement.

193

November

House Flies vs. Cluster Flies

With the imminent arrival of winter, outdoor insect encounters become increasingly rare. When indoors, however, the periodic appearance of flies prevents us from completely forgetting about these winged bugs.

In the North Country, there are two very common species of these familiar household insects which may be seen well into the autumn. First, there is the true house fly, which is active when room temperatures and light conditions are favorable. This insect is most commonly seen walking across a kitchen counter, meandering around a dining room floor, or buzzing about a living room where morsels of food have fallen onto the carpet. Second, there is the cluster fly, which is only active on sunny and unseasonably warm days before winter sets in. This fly tends to congregate around windows, especially those that face south or west, and on the ceiling of rooms where the temperature is a few degrees warmer than it is in the rest of the house.

While these two are nearly identical in appearance, there are a few observable differences between them. When not in flight, the house fly stands slightly higher on its legs than the cluster fly. Also, the wings of the house fly are noticeably transparent and are held outward, thereby giving this fly a distinct triangular shape. The cluster fly folds its wings over its abdomen, which creates a darker image and produces a more elongated body shape.

Unlike nearly all other insects, the house fly attempts to deal with the coming season by taking up residence inside a person's home. Once it gets inside, this fly will scour the home for any morsels of food, especially those that are left unattended. Unwiped kitchen counters, greasy deposits under stoves, and seldom-cleaned gaps behind cabinets where crumbs may occasionally fall are sites that may contain food for this cosmopolitan insect.

In order to perpetuate their existence, a female house fly must find a suitable place in which to deposit her eggs and allow for the development of their larvae and pupa. Uncovered garbage containers and small piles of food that sit undisturbed for several weeks are ideal as breeding sites for this pesky bug.

Since the life span of an adult house fly seldom exceeds one month in summer and three to four months during winter, the individuals that are currently flying about are not the same flies that will appear in the spring.

Adult cluster flies, perhaps surprisingly, actually shy away from coming indoors. They attempt to pass the winter by entering into a dormant state in some protected outdoor spot in which the temperature never drops to the extremes that it can on a calm and clear night during the dead of winter. Ordinarily, as winter approaches, this fly gathers on the exterior walls of a house, particularly ones facing south, or on a roof that is pitched to face the afternoon sun. As evening approaches and the temperature drops, these adults attempt to squeeze through whatever crack or crevice will lead them to a sheltered spot. The spaces inside the eaves of a house, an unheated attic, or inside the partition of an exterior wall are all common over-wintering sites of the cluster fly. There, these flies will huddle together in numbers that may approach one hundred.

Occasionally, while working their way through cracks in walls and roofs or in spaces around a chimney or door, several may accidentally stumble into the living space of the house. In this case, the flies will attempt to locate an avenue back outside. Since the light coming through a window creates the illusion of an access to the outdoors, cluster flies are drawn toward these sites. Eventually, they will exhaust their energy reserves and succumb to the cold that develops around these panes of glass.

By gathering into clusters in various nooks and crannies, these insects are able to conserve body warmth and reduce loss of body moisture to the exceptionally dry winter air. And by experiencing this period of dormancy throughout winter, adult flies can greatly extend their life span into the following spring.

On trips into the attic at this time of year, perhaps to access holiday decorations, you may happen to notice scattered clumps of dark matter attached to a rafter or a ceiling board that, on closer look, prove to be a multitude of brownish-black insect bodies. These are the cluster flies, and they should not be confused with the insects that may be seen sitting on the plate of Christmas cookies which begin showing up on coffee tables around this time of the year.

Quaking Aspen

After the leaves have fallen, it can be quite a challenge to identify deciduous trees and shrubs. Some species, however, posses a unique feature or conspicuous characteristic that makes these woody plants easy to recognize. Such is the case with quaking aspen, also known as the poplar, as this common tree is as easy to identify without its leaves as it is with them.

From the time it becomes a pole-sized sapling until it grows into an oversize tree, the quaking aspen bears a distinct, creamy-white colored bark that may cause it to be mistaken for a white birch by a novice naturalist. However, the birch has a pure white hue to its bark, and with some skill and a knife, its outer covering can be peeled off in a sizeable sheet. (But don't do this to a living birch, as it can harm or kill the tree.) The bark of quaking aspen is a dirtier or more off-white color and cannot be separated from the trunk.

Much of the light color seen on a quaking aspen is caused by a thin deposit of a white, powdery substance that covers its surface. It is believed by some botanists that this substance helps protect the underlying tissue from the harmful ultra-violet rays of the sun, which can be very intense in the open areas preferred by the quaking aspen. As a rule, the more sunlight a poplar is exposed to, the greater the accumulation of this white film and the lighter the color of its trunk and main branches. The bark of aspens that grow on the shores of a lake, pond, or river where the sun's rays can be especially harsh is particularly light. So, too, is the bark of those aspens that grow on south-facing slopes and along stretches of highway that are exposed to the sun throughout the entire day.

Places that receive little direct sunlight are not favored as growing sites by

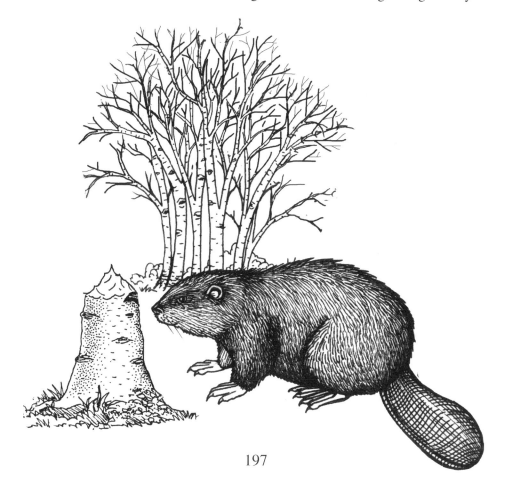

197

this sun-loving tree. This is why the quaking aspen tends to be limited to brushy fields, overgrown meadows, the sides of highways, and other places that are relatively devoid of trees.

Soil quality and depth does not limit the ability of quaking aspen to sprout and take over a site that receives full sunlight. Gravel slopes, rocky hillsides, and sand-laden plains all support stands of poplars provided they are free from the shade of other trees.

During the summer, a quaking aspen can be picked out from other tree species by the unique way in which its leaves flutter, even in a slight breeze. A poplar's foliage is connected to its twigs by means of a flat (rather than most trees' round) leafstalk or petiole. This causes the blade to twist back and forth when it is hit by moving air, rather than being pushed aside, or lifted upward. The resultant shimmering motion of its leaves is quite distinct and can be noticed well away from the tree.

Aside from the aesthetic value it lends to the background, the quaking aspen also provides numerous forms of wildlife with a valuable source of food. Poplar is at the top of the beaver's list of preferred trees, especially during the latter part of autumn when this rodent is busy assembling its winter cache of food, as evidenced by the stumps it leaves behind and the tree species it never touches, regardless of their proximity to the water. To find a quaking aspen, the beaver is known to venture well over a hundred yards from the safety of its pond. Even though cutting up and hauling back an aspen requires a substantial expenditure of effort, the beaver never passes on an opportunity to add this tree's limbs and twigs to its winter food pile.

The ruffed grouse is another animal that depends upon quaking aspen for food. As soon as the forest floor becomes covered with snow, preventing this ground dweller from finding seeds that have fallen earlier in the year, the grouse visits the branches of certain deciduous trees for the buds present on their twigs. During the late afternoon from the end of autumn until early spring, it is not uncommon to see a grouse gingerly stepping on the outer twigs of an aspen in an attempt to pack its crop with as many of the buds as possible.

The varying hare, porcupine, and white-tailed deer are among other mammals that incorporate parts of the aspen into their winter diet. There is also a lengthy list of birds, insects, and various other invertebrates whose lives are directly linked to this tree.

While quaking aspen lacks commercial value, its ability to quickly colonize settings that have been cleared of vegetation makes it invaluable in the process of reestablishing a forest, and its light, creamy-colored bark helps complement the soon-to-form snowy background of a North Country landscape.

Our Two North Country Foxes

The term fox is routinely applied to any small wild canine spotted racing across a road or trotting through a meadow. However, there are two distinctly different species of foxes that reside in the North Country – the red fox and the gray fox – and while striking similarities exist between them, each has its own habits and preferences.

By far the more common species in Northern New York is the red fox, which can be recognized by the white tip on its bushy tail and its more uniformly-colored coat of fur, which is nearly the same shade of rusty-tan as that of a red squirrel. The gray fox, however, also has a noticeable amount of reddish-tan on the lower parts of its sides, which can cause some confusion in identification, although the fur covering its back and the upper portion of its sides is indeed gray. Regardless of the color of its body, the bushy tail of a gray fox has a very dark tip which is fundamental in telling the two species apart.

Aside from a color difference, the winter coat of the red fox is more dense. This increases its insulating value and makes it more suited for life in a colder climate, as do its legs, which are slightly longer than those of its cousin, making it just a little easier for the red fox to travel in places where deep snow often blankets the ground.

Although the red fox is better suited for a life in northern areas, it does not prefer to live in heavily wooded settings (as does the gray fox); instead, it functions best in places where there is a mixture or blend of forests and field. Brushy areas beneath power lines, the borders of agricultural fields and pastures, and the clearings produced during logging operations are all perfect habitats for this wily

canine. Golf courses are also extremely favorable to the red fox, and it is not uncommon to see one of these animals prowling the edge of a fairway, especially late in the afternoon or in the early evening.

The gray fox is more a denizen of the deep woods, particularly those that occur in steep, rocky terrain. Throughout the forests of the southern and central Appalachians, the gray fox reigns as the number one canine. Because this creature has longer, more curved claws, it is better able to scale steep slopes and ridges and grasp the bark of trees with enough force to allow it to climb partway up the trunk. Although it does not do this routinely, as does a raccoon or squirrel, the gray fox will shimmy up a tree in order to get apples, cherries, acorns, or other edibles that are available on the lower limbs near the trunk.

While foxes are commonly thought of as being carnivores, these part-time predators are more correctly labeled as omnivores. Both species in the North Country actually consume substantial amounts of plant matter, especially during the warmer months of the year. From summer through late autumn, berries and seeds comprise a substantial portion of their diets, along with the various small animals and large bugs that they consume.

Since the red fox prefers to prowl open areas, it tends to feed more heavily on the blueberries, raspberries, and blackberries which abound in these settings. The gray fox seems to favor beechnuts, cherries, acorns, and the nuts of hickories. However, since the shortened growing season in the North Country does not favor the development of large stands of oak and hickory trees, the gray fox has much more difficulty obtaining large seeds in this area. Consequently, it often has to find food in areas around towns and villages where fruit trees have been planted, garden vegetables are ripe for the taking, and food scraps discarded by careless humans can be easily acquired.

Even in densely forested settings, the red fox far outnumbers the gray in the subarctic climate that prevails throughout the North Country. Should you happen to catch a glimpse of a fox, but not know for sure which species you're looking at, look to the tail.

The Coydog

The term "coydog" is frequently applied to the breed of coyote that commonly resides throughout the Adirondacks. Because this wild canid is larger than the coyote of the West and exhibits some different behaviors, some people assumed it was a crossbreed between a coyote and a dog when it first appeared in northern New York during the 1940's. The word coydog was coined – and has stuck – despite an overwhelming amount of scientific evidence that such a crossbreed would not be able to perpetuate its race in the wilds.

Individuals who were successful breeding a coyote with a dog in captivity discovered that the products of such a mating encounter are unable to reproduce effectively in the wilds. Rather than becoming fertile during late January or in early February, like a coyote or wolf, a coydog comes into heat sometime from mid-November to the first week of December. This displaced heat cycle prevents the female from finding a male capable of mating with her. Unlike a male domestic dog which can mate at any time, a wild male canid is only able to produce sperm during a limited period in midwinter, which overlaps with the time when the female comes into heat.

In the unlikely case that a female coydog encounters an animal during the late autumn that is capable of servicing her reproductive needs, the birth of her pups will occur sometime from mid-January through early February. This time during midwinter is when our weather tends to be at its worst and food is most scarce. These two factors combine to greatly reduce the pups' chances for survival. Since the coyote and wolf don't breed until midwinter, their pups are not born until early spring, when conditions are greatly improved.

Coyote and wolf researchers have also observed that both parents are needed to successfully raise a litter of pups in the wilds. Since a domestic male dog never remains with the female after a reproductive encounter, the job of creating dens, finding food, and tending to the needs of the pups falls solely on the female. The chance that a single canid parent could rear a litter of pups is extremely low, even during the spring when the weather is more favorable and hunting conditions are substantially better. Should a coydog be successful in mating, the high mortality rate of the pups would prevent virtually all from reaching maturity.

The coyote that exists throughout the North Country is properly referred to as the eastern coyote and, at the present time, is considered to be a separate subspecies of its western relative. The fact that our coyote is larger and tends to prey on bigger game than its western counterpart is believed by some naturalists to be a response to living in our northern climate. Creatures that inhabit colder regions are bigger, as this helps them to better retain body heat.

During the winter, when deep powder and crusty snow conditions occur, this opportunistic hunter is forced to prey on whatever will supply it with the greatest amount of food. Because white-tailed deer congregate in lowland forests, they often become the easiest animal to locate and catch in many sections of the North Country. This switch to big game animals from smaller ones has favored larger and more powerful coyotes over smaller ones. Through the process of natural selection, these larger coyotes have been the ones that have been the most successful in reproducing their genetic stock. By forming small packs during the winter, at the time when deer become a staple in the their diet, the coyotes further ensure their ecological success.

Another theory that is often put forth to explain the differences between western coyotes and the ones in this region is the possible presence of wolf genes in our population. Since coyotes and wolves have nearly identical breeding seasons, it is possible that lone wolves mated with coyotes at some point in time, either as they spread eastward or after they arrived in northern New York.

Research is ongoing into the pedigree of the eastern coyote. It may be that this animal is indeed a subspecies of coyote, or it's possible it could be a cross between a coyote and a wolf. Some people speculate that if wolf genes are incorporated into our coyote, they are those of the red wolf, which formerly occupied the eastern portion of the country, rather than the gray wolf, which is widely distributed across northern and western regions. In any event, since World War II, a resourceful predator has gradually become well established throughout the North Country, and although it is still often referred to as a coydog, that is not what it is.

The Importance of Fat

As a rule, all forms of animal life in northern regions spend the vast majority of their time from the late summer through the autumn engaging in only one activity – eating. Regardless of whether they remain active in winter, retreat into some shelter to sleep away the coming season, or migrate to a much warmer climate, all creatures develop a strong urge at this time of the year to consume as much food as possible.

Building a layer of fat is essential for warm-blooded animals as it enables them to retain body heat. Because of its low density, fat has a correspondingly low level of thermal conductivity, so as it forms just below the skin, it acts as a blanket. The more of this light-colored cellular tissue an animal develops, the easier it becomes for that creature to hold in the heat it produces when it oxidizes its food. For example, the insulating layer of fat on a polar bear and musk ox is so effective that these two large mammals often fail to melt the snow beneath them when they bed down. In a similar way, the loon can sit in near-freezing water for weeks without becoming chilled because of the fat that forms on its belly. For creatures that exist in arctic and subarctic climates, fat is as much a necessity as is a thick covering of fur or feathers.

Individuals that fail to build an insulating layer of fat dissipate body heat at a faster rate. This forces them to burn more food in an attempt to maintain an appropriate internal temperature. Lean creatures are always at a greater risk of suffering from hypothermia, especially during those occasions when severe weather conditions limit their ability to feed. Young animals, inexperienced at finding food, may fail to develop an adequate fat reserve in the autumn. Sick and injured individuals are likewise inclined to be without appropriate amounts of fat going into the winter. Consequently, it is these creatures that are vulnerable to hypothermia and most likely to perish as the cold becomes more intense and lasts for increasing periods of time.

For migratory birds, it is fat reserves that fuel prolonged bouts of flight. Although most birds do not appear to be overly stout in the late summer and autumn before they depart the region, all birds must develop a substantial deposit of fat as the days become shorter. In some species, fat may comprise 35 to 40 percent of their pre-migration weight.

Even cold-blooded animals such as frogs and snakes, and bugs that pass the winter as adults, develop fat by eating more food than they burn during the time prior to becoming dormant. This concentration of fat in their cells lowers the temperature at which the water within them will freeze. While water solidifies at 32 degrees under normal conditions, this freezing point becomes lower when certain molecules are present, enabling creatures like the spring peeper and toad to lower their own freezing point so that the moisture in their bodies remains in a liquid form despite being cooled to temperatures in the 20s.

For many people, Thanksgiving marks the start of a month-long season characterized by an endless desire to nibble on cookies, cakes, pies, and other holiday treats. While frequent visits to the refrigerator may not be the healthiest of practices at other times of the year, the urge to fill one's mouth with food is possibly an instinctive reaction or natural response to the coming of winter. Since we have evolved under the same environmental conditions as other forms of animal life, our need for another portion of potatoes and gravy and urge to gnaw on that other drumstick becomes more understandable.

It must also be emphasized that the resolution to shed those extra (yet necessary) pounds after the start of the New Year also has ecological merit. By the time early January arrives, all animals are beginning to rely on their accumulated fat (and not the intake of food) to help meet their energy demands. Given this proven scientific fact, and in accordance with the spirit of the season, one should never dwell on the negative aspect of fat until a week after Christmas.

Hibernation vs. Prolonged Sleep

To most people, the term "hibernation" has come to represent the dormant period experienced by all animals that are inactive throughout the colder months of the year. Among wildlife biologists, however, this word has a much more specific meaning, and it does not apply to every creature that passes the winter in an unconscious state.

Biologically, hibernation is a profound quiescent stage in which a creature's overall metabolism drops significantly. During this deeply depressed physiological state, the individual's body temperature often falls dozens of degrees and may settle at a level that is nearly equal to that of its surroundings.

This is the situation with the species of bats which overwinter in North Country caves and abandoned mine shafts that extend deeply underground. In sections of these subterranean shelters, the temperature may be a very consistent fifty degrees or more throughout the winter. Although bats typically maintain a body temperature of slightly over one hundred degrees in summer, these creatures find it impossible to generate that level of heat during the many months in which food is totally absent. Since weight restricts the amount of fat these delicate flying creatures are able to build before winter, they are forced to limit their rate of oxidation until midspring. Consequently, after reaching a suitable hibernating site, bats greatly reduce their metabolism to a level that barely keeps them alive. This results in a drop of body temperature by some forty to fifty degrees. Since their thin coat of hair does not allow them to retain much of the warmth generated by food oxidation, they must seek out a place that remains at a temperature favorable to their systems. Occasionally, bats cluster together in a further attempt to retain the limited amount of metabolic heat that is produced during their state of hibernation.

Similarly, jumping mice are too small to build more than several grams of body fat in summer. These creatures are also forced to reduce their metabolic rate, causing their internal temperature to plummet. Unlike bats, jumping mice in

the North Country cannot let their body temperature reach a thermal equilibrium with that of their surroundings. Because these common rodents spend the winter in burrows that often fail to remain below the frost line, jumping mice must generate enough warmth to prevent themselves from literally freezing to death, and because of their solitary existence, there are no other warm bodies in the burrow with which to snuggle or share body warmth.

The depressed state of hibernation experienced by the jumping mouse in the winter also reduces its need for oxygen. As the ground freezes, the ability of oxygen to permeate the soil decreases. Since the burrow entrance that leads to the surface is plugged to prevent other critters from wandering in and threatening the jumping mouse while it is unconscious, the level of oxygen can drop drastically if it is consumed at too high a rate. In this respect, hibernation prevents the likelihood of suffocation.

Bears, raccoons, and skunks all will enter into a period of dormancy over the course of the next several weeks; however, these more sizeable mammals do not experience a true hibernation. When these creatures curl up in their dens during the late autumn, they merely fall asleep, without experiencing a major reduction in their metabolic rate. Because all of these animals have the ability to haul around a thick, insulating layer of fat and a dense coat of fur, they are able to maintain a near normal internal temperature throughout the winter season without much difficulty. Also, because the dens of these animals are open to the air, they never experience a shortage of oxygen while confined to their sleeping chambers.

Although all of these larger animals experience numerous physiological changes as they enter their prolonged period of sleep, none result in a drastic lowering of their body temperature as in the case of the bats, jumping mice, chipmunks, and woodchucks.

So while it is common to hear that bears and raccoons are beginning to hibernate, in correct biological terms neither enters this type of dormancy. They are, rather, simply starting an unconscious period that more closely resembles sleep, except for the fact that it will probably last for at least the next four or five months.

The Wild Turkey

It wasn't that long ago that the only wild turkeys that were seen in the North Country were on Thanksgiving decorations and centerpieces. However, in recent years, this familiar game bird can be regularly observed along the sides of roads and in fields, meadows, and woodlands all across our region, including the Central Adirondacks.

It is believed that the wild turkey was non-existent in the North Country prior to the 1800s. As forests were cleared for farming in the valleys and logging devastated the woodlands in the mountains, the land became totally unsuitable for this part-time forest dweller, and unregulated hunting practices during this period were responsible for the complete elimination of this meaty game bird from the entire state and most areas in the East. With the conversion of small family farms back into forests and the dawn of the era of conservation, conditions for the turkey slowly started to improve, and sometime after World War II, the turkey began to reappear in the southernmost sections of New York State. With the help of several wildlife agencies, this large game bird has been successful in greatly expanding its range northwards, and it is now a permanent resident of places that never supported it before.

The patchwork of forests, agricultural fields, and brushy wastelands that have been created throughout much of our region have benefited the turkey's resurgence. During mid-spring, the female, also known as the hen, requires an area of dense cover for her nest, which is nothing more than a slight depression in a secluded spot surrounded by thick vegetation. After the eggs hatch, the young birds, referred to as poults, begin a period of devouring any and all bugs that live on the ground. These invertebrates are rich in the proteins required to produce the turkey's large body size. Ordinarily, open areas seem to harbor the greatest concentration of such soil-dwelling organisms. Forest edges are also regularly frequented, as these settings provide both food and cover into which the poults can scatter should a predator like a fox, coyote, or bobcat happen to stray into the area.

Toward the end of the summer and during the autumn, as the crop of cherries, maple and ash keys (often referred to as "helicopters"), beechnuts, and acorns fall to the ground, the wild turkey gravitates toward stands of these deciduous trees. Families typically merge at this time of year, forming flocks that can reach several dozen in number. While they may still visit open areas, especially if cultivated crops have recently been harvested or when the seeds of various grasses and weeds are abundant, the mast of trees gradually becomes the staple item in their diet.

Even though hardwoods provide the best feeding sites, stands of softwood become critically important to turkeys as winter sets in. Like deer, the wild turkey uses favorable lowland forests dominated by evergreens in an attempt to escape the blustery winds and deep snow that would be lethal in exposed settings. Unlike the grouse, which has toes suited for walking on snow, the feet of the turkey do not function well under these conditions. Since snow doesn't accumulate as much under the boughs of conifers, and it also packs better there, it provides a

210

more appealing travel surface for the turkey.

Finding food often becomes a problem in the North Country, especially in snow belt regions, yet a healthy turkey is able to go without eating if harsh conditions prohibit it from leaving its roost. It is reported that a turkey can survive up to two full weeks without eating before it begins to suffer from hypothermia. The large body size of the turkey, along with its layer of fat and dense covering of plumage, makes its heat retention capabilities excellent. The lack of feathers on its head, which helps to characterize the turkey, does not greatly reduce its rate of cooling, since its head is far smaller in comparison to its body, and the turkey has the ability to draw it in close to its body to reduce heat loss.

Despite a high level of mortality in winter, the wild turkey continues to thrive in this region. Climate changes that have occurred over the past centuries have allowed this bird, along with numerous other forms of wildlife, to expand their geographic range further north than during the period when the Pilgrims began arriving on this continent. The turkey is an unmistakable symbol of the Thanksgiving season, and among the many things that we should be thankful for is the healthy environment that has allowed for its reestablishment throughout our region.

The Rare Spruce Grouse

While it is fairly safe to assume that any grouse you see in the North Country is a ruffed grouse, care should be taken in coming to such a conclusion when this type of wild fowl is spotted in a sizeable boreal forest. It is here that the rarely seen spruce grouse can be found, residing in scattered pockets of black spruce and balsam fir that are reminiscent of those that cover much of northern Canada and Alaska.

A boreal forest is a unique type of ecological setting that tends to be located in lowlands where the terrain is relatively flat, the soil is very moist and high in tannic acid, and cold air regularly becomes entrapped over the immediate area. Although several species of spruce can exist under these conditions, along with various other conifers and selected species of deciduous trees, it is the black

211

spruce and balsam fir that dominate this forest.

Within a boreal forest, the
ground often contains spongy
masses of sphagnum moss and
scattered clumps of shrubs
belonging to the heath family of
plants. These shrubs, such as
Labrador tea, leatherleaf, and the
laurels and azaleas, are characterized by the tough, green
leaves present on their twigs
throughout the winter. They are
especially abundant in places in
which the trees are not closely
packed, with periodic breaks in
the canopy that allow for some
sunlight to sweep across the forest floor during the day.

In areas where the trees have reached maturity, or where many trees grow
very close together, the canopy can become quite thick. The near total lack of
sunlight reaching the ground creates a forest community devoid of all ground
vegetation, except for an occasional cluster of mushrooms in the carpet of dead,
decaying needles.

While it prefers more open woodlands, the spruce grouse can also exist in
these denser boreal settings, as it is well suited for a life among these conifers.
Even though both species of grouse feed primarily on tree buds from late autumn
through mid-spring, the spruce grouse strongly prefers the tips of various conifers,
while the ruffed grouse favors those of certain hardwoods, particularly aspens.
Thus, the type of tree upon which a grouse is seen nibbling, especially in the late
afternoon, may be used as a clue in distinguishing between these two birds.

Another difference between them is the way they respond to the presence
of humans. Since expanses of black spruce and fir forests are not likely to be
frequented by people, the spruce grouse has not yet developed the wary nature of

its more often seen and hunted cousin. Consequently, it is possible to approach one of these northern birds to within a few feet before it will flush. This lack of fear has earned it the name "fool's hen" in those locations in the far north where it can still be hunted.

Because of their similar size and coloration, it is quite difficult to distinguish between these two species of grouse by looks alone, especially when only catching a brief glimpse of one, or in poor light. If a clean view is obtained, however, the profile of the bird's head and tail, along with the presence of some subtle colored markings, can be used to make a positive identification.

When the ruffed grouse moves into semi-open places, and whenever it senses danger, it instinctively alters its plumage by causing the feathers on top of its head to form a small yet noticeable crest. The spruce grouse lacks this distinctive feature. Also, the tail of the ruffed grouse appears slightly longer and has a broad black band near its end.

Overall, the spruce grouse possesses darker plumage compared to that of its tan, gray, and brown relative. The male spruce grouse also has a small red patch just above its eyes, which is unlike that of any other species of grouse. Additionally, the legs of the spruce grouse are covered by a thicker and fluffier layer of feathers that provides increased protection against the colder climate to which this bird is typically exposed.

In the early 1800s, before the vast stands of softwoods that covered a majority of the North Country, particularly the Adirondacks, were devastated, the spruce grouse was believed to be fairly common. Presently, the limited number of boreal forests in the region are able to support only very small and isolated populations of this unique ground dweller. The relative inaccessibility of boreal forests, and the difficulty one would have traveling through them, prevents hikers from very often visiting these remote stretches of wilderness.

Efforts are being made to expand area covered by boreal forests and increase the population of the spruce grouse. Yet, regardless of the amount of time and energy put into this endeavor, it is highly unlikely that the spruce grouse will ever come to enjoy the same success as that of the wild turkey. Consequently, as you travel throughout our region, it is safe to assume that if you see one of these members of the pheasant family, it will be the ruffed grouse.

Crows

When it comes to animal behavior and response to environmental situations, the crow is considered to be as complex and versatile as any bird. While most types of birds react in a similar, if not identical, way to the same set of circumstances, the crow may not, for this jet black bird is, at times, as individualistic as humans.

During the spring and summer breeding season, crows live in a family that can vary from only an adult male, a female, and nestlings to a much larger collection of related individuals. On occasion, offspring from previous nesting seasons join the adults to help with the chores associated with rearing a brood, and some extended family members may construct their nests nearby, forming a small community. The crows' social nature also extends to their attempts at locating food, defending against natural enemies, and dealing with the change in seasons.

The response of crows to the approach of winter can vary greatly. Some individuals migrate far to the south to a more favorable climate, while some fly to locations within the North Country where the snow does not accumulate as much as in our snow belt regions. Other crows elect to reside in the same general location in winter as they did during the summer and autumn. And it has been noted that what an individual crow may elect to do one winter may not necessarily be its action for the next.

The hardy individuals that stay in the North Country for the winter typically congregate into flocks during the late afternoon at a central roost. This communal nightly retreat is situated in a spot that is sheltered from the prevailing northwesterly winds and tends to be exposed to the morning sun. By coming together to rest, these individuals are better protected against a sneak attack by a predator. Some researchers also believe this enables them to communicate to one another about the location of temporary food sources, and to alert each other when traditional feeding areas are no longer worthwhile. From these roosts, the birds fan out shortly after sunrise towards areas with which they are familiar.

Unlike other perching birds that are permanent residents of the North Country, crows are not drawn toward bird feeders. Their intelligence and their ability to learn a variety of new behaviors has allowed them to develop feeding tactics that are well suited for living in both rural and suburban settings. These part-time scavengers, garbage pickers, field foragers, and road kill connoisseurs rely on keen eyesight and a knowledge of the area to locate a wide variety of more substantive items to consume. The familiar cawing call of a crow is believed to relay information about an individual's success or failure to locate food to other crows.

Despite the crow's abundance in populated areas and its rather high profile, much still remains unknown about the lives of these large and often noisy creatures. The extremely wary personality of these black birds makes observing of them difficult. While most birds can be approached closely for study under certain situations or during various times of the year, crows always seem to be on the alert for humans, and they never tolerate a nearby person watching their

every move. This is why a scarecrow can occasionally be effective in discouraging these birds from disturbing crops. However, most crows are able to soon figure out if a human-like object is artificial and poses no threat, or if it is real and should be avoided.

Attempting to distinguish one crow from another is yet another challenge that confronts the naturalists studying their behavior. Although the personality of these birds is said to be of value in identifying the members of a flock, even minute differences in their plumage are practically non-existent – and therefore almost useless in singling out individual birds. Consequently, it becomes exceptionally difficult for a researcher to positively recognize various individuals and determine their roles in the social organization within the flock.

It has been stated by one bird researcher that while crows are among our most familiar birds, far less is known about them than about birds that are as rare as the California Condor.

Ravens

North Country winters are not kind to the animals that remain in the region year-round, and the raven is one creature that takes full advantage of the havoc this season wreaks on the young, sick, and old members of our wildlife community.

The raven is an accomplished scavenger that has evolved the ability to locate the remains of animals that have succumbed to the rigors of the season or met their demise in a confrontation with a predator. Its highly efficient style of flight allows the raven to cover vast areas of wilderness to scan for carrion, and its keen sense of sight is able to recognize the shape and form of deceased creatures amid the dormant vegetation. Additionally, its eyes are well adapted for detecting the blood which occurs around a fatally wounded animal.

When it sees a coyote, bobcat, fox, or fisher on the move during the day, the raven is known to follow the predator from the air in an attempt to locate any unconsumed meat it may leave unattended. Since these carnivores have an exceptionally keen sense of smell, they are far better able to sniff out the remains

216

of victims of the winter that have become entombed in the snow than most other birds. It is also believed that the raven may alert a pack of coyotes to the presence of a deer or fox that has bedded down close by. In this way, the raven is sure to get its fill of leftovers should a kill be made.

Because its bill is unable to tear through the hide of a deer or other tough-skinned creature, the raven must wait for an animal with sharp canine teeth or a heavy, hooked bill to rip open a carcass. Once the underlying flesh has been exposed, the raven can feast on it, as its bill is capable of cleaning every shred of edible matter from both bone and skin. Even carrion that is frozen solid can be consumed by the raven, provided the overlying hide has been adequately pulled or gnawed off.

When a small, dead animal such as a varying hare or red squirrel is found with its body already torn open, perhaps on the side of a highway, a single raven or two will devour the remains as inconspicuously as possible. This is done so as not to alert other ravens that might happen to be in the vicinity. But if a

much larger piece of animal matter such as a recently killed deer is discovered, the finder will notify other ravens within the general region that a feast is available. Researchers have noted that word of such a find, which is communicated by emitting a specific call, spreads quickly among the raven community, and that individuals from as far away as fifty miles may be at the site the next morning to ensure that nothing goes to waste.

In appearance, the raven can easily be confused with the crow, as these closely related species are nearly identical in shape and possess the same jet black color, but the raven is nearly twice the size of its avian cousin and has a notably deeper and raspier cawing call. While it is often hard to evaluate the size of a bird when it is in flight or sitting on a guard rail some distance away, the voice of a raven is distinct, as it sounds like a crow with a very bad cold or sore throat, and its volume is slightly higher.

The raven's style of flight can also be used to identify this denizen of the far north. Crows tend to fly in a straight line and exhibit a continuous and rhymic wing beat. In contrast, the raven occasionally soars and glides and appears more graceful when in flight. Because of the long distance it travels in search of carrion, the raven has evolved the ability to take advantage of thermals and other favorable air currents. Also, the raven may be seen changing directions in a swooping and almost acrobatic manner. The crow is very deliberate in its aerial travels and seldom deviates from its direct, forward flight path.

While the raven does exhibit some social tendencies, it frequently goes in search of food alone. Occasionally, a pair of ravens may be seen sailing above a ridgeline, circling near a cliff, or cruising along a stretch of highway; however, this bird is seldom seen in the sizeable flocks of the crow.

Winter in the North Country is a very difficult time for all forms of animal life. While most meat eaters will scavenge if the opportunity arises, the raven has evolved the skills for making its living entirely on the misfortune of other members of our wildlife community.

The Pine Marten

The pine marten, a little-known member of the weasel family that is widely distributed across the northernmost forests of the world, lives in the upper-elevation forests of the Adirondacks, where winter is long and far more severe than in the surrounding valleys. This sleek inhabitant of the Great North Woods is more at home in the tops of trees than on the ground and often fails to run away on those rare occasions when a chance encounter with a human occurs.

Known to old-time trappers and backwoodsmen as the sable, the pine marten is slightly longer and lankier than a gray squirrel, and it can be recognized, in part, by its rather conspicuous ears. Throughout Siberia, in most of Alaska, and across northern Canada, this animal bears a rich, chocolate-colored fur that is used in the making of sable coats, stoles, and other high-priced articles of outerwear. In this section of its geographic range, however, the marten tends to be a rust-tan color that is only a few shades darker than that of a red squirrel. The lighter colored fur of our martens is not viewed with favor by those that relish rich apparel.

The dense stands of spruce and fir that cover many North Country areas above 3000 feet in elevation are the primary haunt of the pine marten. This arboreal weasel is also known to inhabit large-scale boreal forests that cover lowland areas in which cold air regularly becomes trapped.

In these settings, the marten routinely prowls the canopy for red squirrels. With an agility among the boughs of the evergreens that is second to none, the marten is often able to outmaneuver this common rodent. Occasionally, red squirrels will elude the marten by seeking refuge inside a cavity within a tree that is too small for the marten to enter or by ducking into a narrow burrow under the snow.

The marten also preys on flying squirrels, varying hare, mice, voles, grouse, and numerous songbirds. For much of the day and during the evening, this patient predator sits quietly on a limb that affords a good view of the ground below. Runways used by the snowshoe rabbit are especially sought out, as are places in which a grouse may forage. When one of these animals eventually ventures beneath it, the marten will pounce in an attempt to make a kill.

Yet despite its relative abundance in the High Peaks of the Adirondacks and its expanding numbers in conifer-covered lowlands in the Park, the marten is not a commonly sighted creature. Since it does not move around much and makes very little noise, the marten does not normally attract much attention to its presence. As a result, a hiker who is concentrating more on where he or she is stepping than on what may be on a limb above will likely pass the marten by without ever noticing it.

Another reason that the marten is rarely observed is that, in spite of its numbers in the region, it has a relatively low population density. Unlike the chipmunk or red squirrel, which can number well into the hundreds of individuals per

square mile of favorable habitat, it is estimated that not more than two martens are able to exist in an area of similar size.

Since the marten does not normally encounter many people, and most individuals simply pass it by without ever disturbing it, this weasel has not developed a very strong sense of repulsion for humans. On those rare occasions when a marten happens to be spotted, it may simply continue to sit where it is without immediately getting up and scampering away.

It is generally not easy to walk the trails that cut through those sections of Adirondack forests that are more reminiscent of the far north than of a temperate climate. Uneven ground on precariously pitched slopes, frequent boulders, and in the late fall and winter, patches of ice, all combine to force travelers in this boreal zone to focus all of their attention on where they are stepping. Occasionally though, an individual will look up and happen to notice one of these sleek, tan-colored weasels staring down. This is the marten, one animal that has not yet learned to fear humans, which is exceptional for this day and age.

Evening Grosbeaks

It is ordinarily during the latter part of autumn or very early winter that the migration of evening grosbeaks peaks in the North Country. After abandoning its summer breeding territories in the far north and in the spruce-fir forests at upper elevations in the Adirondacks, this colorful bird arrives at its wintering area just as the seasons change. Large tracts of conifer forests in lowlands and valleys serve as a home to these gregarious birds if the cones on the softwood trees support an adequate supply of seeds. If not, the evening grosbeak is known to descend in sizeable flocks upon towns and villages, where there are numerous, closely-spaced homes that maintain feeders stocked with sunflower seeds.

As below-zero readings become more common, the evening grosbeak, along with all other birds, experiences an increased demand for nourishment to maintain an appropriate internal body temperature. Yet, because autumn's gales have

stripped the keys from the maples, along with the mast from other hardwoods, a near total lack of natural food develops in our deciduous forests, when the blanket of snow that usually begins to form at this time of the year prevents access to the seeds that have previously fallen on the ground. In order for these seed eaters to remain alive, they must either locate a stand of conifers which are rich in cones containing their tiny, winged seeds, or travel to an area in which sunflower seeds are readily available.

Like all members of the finch family, the evening grosbeak possesses a short yet heavy bill that is adapted for cracking open the shuck that covers seeds. The effectiveness of its mandibles may be seen when this bird visits a feeder containing sunflower seeds. With only a few powerful contractions of its jaw, this stout-bodied bird has the seed casing split and the enclosed kernel of food removed and swallowed. Its bill also enables it to pry open the scales of pine, spruce, and fir cones in order to access these natural food sources.

The bright yellow, black, and white colors of the male grosbeak, which make this bird easy to identify, are believed by ornithologists to be a defense that draws attention away from nearby females, which are more dull and drab in appearance. Should a predator like a pine marten or goshawk happen to detect a flock of grosbeaks, it would be a male that would most likely be spotted first and targeted. This is why the male is instinctively more wary. When one bird quickly flees from its feeding spot, all of the other males, in a reflex response, will also take to the air and fly to a place of greater cover. While some females may immediately take off, others may remain in order to prevent attention from being drawn toward them as they scramble to leave the scene. After carefully assessing the situation, the remaining females will either remain motionless in the hopes that the predator will overlook their presence, quickly exit the area along with the other members of the flock, or simply continue to feed on the seeds should the incident be deemed a false alarm.

A century and a half ago, before the era of bird feeders, the evening grosbeak lived only in the mountains of western North America. As people gradually discovered the pleasure of watching birds just outside a window during the winter, feeders began to increase in popularity. This allowed the range of the evening grosbeak to expand eastward, as it now exists throughout the northern portions of our country, all the way to the Atlantic coast.

As winter's grip on our region becomes more intense, an ever-increasing number of birds begin to appear at feeders, and a raucous flock of evening grosbeaks may be among the visitors. While some people dislike their pushy manners and habit of consuming every last morsel at a feeder, other individuals enjoy watching them munch on seeds and interact with one another in their loosely knit flock. Their presence is unpredictable, however, since the winter flocks of evening grosbeaks have a nomadic tendency, and their arrival in early winter and departure in the spring rarely happens at the same time from year to year. Still, chances are good that there will always be a few of these noisy birds around if a feeder with an abundance of sunflower seeds is maintained throughout this season.

Cedar

Along with being used by humans as a decoration during the holiday season, the leafy boughs of the northern white cedar serve as a vital source of nourishment to numerous members of our wildlife community, especially during the bleak months of winter.

For leaf-eating creatures like the white-tailed deer and varying hare, autumn is the start of a difficult period. The total absence of succulent vegetation at this time of year causes these herbivores to find sustenance in the fibrous tips of certain hardwood twigs. Although conifer needles, fronds of ferns that remain green throughout the year, and clumps of luxuriant moss are attractive in appearance, the unacceptable texture of these plants and their lack of digestible matter places them on the list of low-priority food items. However, the soft, scale-like greenery that develops on cedar twigs is much more palatable, and it contains a rich array of the nutrients that can be absorbed by the digestive system of these common forms of wildlife. Some deer researchers have estimated that an adult whitetail needs only four pounds of cedar browse per day during the winter to maintain a good state of health, as compared to the five pounds of hardwood buds it would require.

The deer's affinity for cedar can be illustrated by the browse line it creates on these trees. Inevitably, wherever both cedar and deer exist, tree limbs are completely devoid of all foliage up to the height that a deer can reach, which is roughly four to five feet above the ground. Since many lakes throughout the North Country are rimmed with cedar, this browse line can be seen when looking at the vegetation along the shore.

One compound present in the greenery of cedar that is of value to humans is vitamin C. Centuries ago, Native American tribes made a broth from the most-recently formed scales that occur at the ends of each foliage cluster in their effort to obtain this important substance. According to legend, the crew of Jacques Cartier, the explorer who established France's claim to sections of North America, developed scurvy during the winter of 1542. This was the first time that

Cartier attempted to remain in the New World for an entire year, and the site he chose for his encampment was very near present-day Quebec City. The inhabitants of that area recognized this vitamin-deficient condition and provided all the expedition members with a cedar broth. Eventually they recovered, and when he returned to France, Cartier brought several white cedar seedlings with him. Historians believe that this was the first time that a plant from North America was introduced into Europe. In France and several other areas, northern white cedar is properly referred to as arbor vitae, or tree of life. This name is said to have originated from Cartier's life-restoring encounter with this tree.

Along with serving as a source of food, dense stands of cedar trees provide many winter birds with shelter during our long winter nights. At sunset, birds retreat to those places that afford them the greatest protection from the wind. Be-

cause cedar grows in lowland settings where the wind is always less intense than at higher elevations, birds seek out these sites in which to roost as dusk approaches. Additionally, the boughs of cedar fail to cluster together in the way the needles of pines do when the temperature drops well below zero. This allows for a more extensive layer of cover that protects them from the wind and from being seen by predators.

At this time of year, evergreen foliage may be commonly seen in wreaths, garlands, and other decorations. While some of this greenery may be slightly more fragrant, easier to obtain, and more traditional in its use at Christmas than cedar is, none impacts as favorably on our wildlife community or has such a rich history as the tree of life.

225

Reindeer and Caribou

No form of animal life is as closely tied to Christmas as the reindeer, the cold-hardy creatures of the far north that are pictured every time Santa is shown in his sleigh. While known as reindeer in popular stories and throughout Scandinavia and northern Russia, this member of the deer family is more commonly referred to in North America as caribou, which is a French-Canadian word for reindeer.

Throughout the world, there are several subspecies or breeds of this familiar mammal, each with its own habitat preference and behavioral characteristics. Christmas experts have not been able to agree upon which breed is employed by Santa for his epic trip around the planet.

The barren-ground caribou is the best known member of this species and the one that most people think of when the term caribou is mentioned. It lives in massive, nomadic herds which travel from the northern sections of the arctic in summer to the southern fringe of the tundra in winter in a large-scale migration that is occasionally the subject of nature programs or wildlife documentaries. Residing in an area that stretches from Alaska to the western shores of Hudson Bay, it is the most highly migratory of all forms of terrestrial mammals. And because it is capable of traversing such enormous expanses of territory, it is the one that some people believe is used to pull Santa's sleigh.

Peary's caribou is another breed of this animal. It is slightly smaller than other reindeer and is better adapted for tolerating the cold, harsh living conditions that exist in the far north. Peary's caribou inhabits the northernmost islands which dot the Arctic Ocean, as well as the northern shores of Greenland. Because it can survive in regions that are so close to the North Pole, where, as everyone knows, Santa lives, there are those who believe that this is the type of reindeer used by the jolly old elf.

The woodland caribou, the largest of the reindeer breeds, lives further south in northern North America. It lives in much smaller herds than its very close cousins, and a herd of eight or nine individuals is not uncommon. It prefers an existence in more wooded settings, as it frequently takes up residence in the boreal forests that stretch across sections of Canada. Many centuries ago, the North Country was also covered with such vast stands of softwood trees, and scientists believe that small herds of woodland caribou once roamed throughout our area, especially during the period following the retreat of the last glaciers.

Unlike the more northern breeds, woodland caribou are not highly migratory, and on occasion, they may remain in one general area when food is abundant there. By providing them with an adequate amount of edible matter, a person such as Santa might be able to maintain a small herd, keeping them in one area all year. Also, unlike the two types of reindeer previously mentioned, which

graze heavily on lichens and small arctic grasses and weeds, this type of caribou is more of a browser. The buds of trees and the foliage of certain evergreens are important items in its diet. Occasionally, it is known to paw at the ground with its large hooves in order to uncover the roots of small ground plants. It is this breed of reindeer that would find a few carrots placed out in a strategic spot to be a real treat.

The breed of caribou that evolved in the far northern reaches of Europe and western Asia is the one properly known as the reindeer. This animal was domesticated thousands of years ago by the nomadic inhabitants of these areas. Many have been trained to pull sleighs and are quite accustomed to being around people. For these reasons it is reported that European reindeer are the ones used at Christmastime, although critics contend that since Santa has the ability to establish a positive rapport with any wild beast, including other breeds of caribou, he could easily convince any or all of them to pull his sleigh.

Anyone with a discerning eye for wildlife who is fortunate enough to see these creatures on Christmas Eve might have a slim chance of determining which breed of caribou transports Santa around the earth. However, the physical differences among these subspecies are quite subtle, and since it is quite dark when those annual visits are made, it would be nearly impossible to assess their exact identity. Seeing Santa's reindeer well enough to allow for their positive identification would indeed be a magical moment.

Bog Lemmings

In locations as different as back yards, large pastures, and wilderness forests, it is not uncommon for the casual observer to notice small, round openings in the ground or exposed sections of tunnels that run just below the soil's surface. While moles and voles are responsible for the creation of these subterranean passageways in most North Country settings, the bog lemming is another animal of our region that produces and lives in such burrows. In bogs and in certain types of woodland swamps, this southern variety of lemming maintains similar tunnels through the soil.

Like the lemmings of the arctic, bog lemmings are small, mouse-sized rodents that have a fairly large, rounded head and small eyes and ears. Because these mammals, like moles and voles, must spend much of their time pushing their way through tunnels with very small diameters, large, protruding append-ages on their head would interfere with their ability to squeeze through those nar-row passageways. These critters, therefore, have evolved a good sense of hearing without the need for large ears, such as those of mice.

The lemmings are identified, in part, by short, stubby tails which are only about one-eighth the length of their bodies, or roughly the same length as their hind legs. In the North Country, only the pine vole has a tail that is of compa-rable length, but the lemming has a coat of denser, shaggier fur. Since lemmings ordinarily reside in sub-arctic and arctic environments, their fur must afford them adequate protection against the cold.

While bogs are its preferred habitat, this lemming is also known to take up residence along the edges of swampy woods, especially those with a scattering of deciduous trees. Any settings in which the climate is cool, the soil is soft and moist, and where sunlight is able to reach the ground and sustain the growth of

large clumps of weeds, sedges, grasses, mosses, and ferns are likely to be inhab-ited by this mammal. Because of the meadow vole's dominance of open sites in drier locations, the bog lemming tends to be limited to those places in which its slightly larger and more aggressive cousin is unable to exist.

Unlike all of the other species of small rodents that occur in the North Coun-try, the bog lemming does not exhibit omnivorous feeding habits. Rather, this chisel-toothed critter dines almost exclusively on plant matter. Seeds, berries, and especially the succulent parts of plants compose the bulk of its diet. And while it is known to occasionally consume bugs, the bog lemming's intake of such invertebrate matter is minimal compared to that of its relatives.

Throughout late autumn and early winter, the bog lemming is busy creating caches of food in places that are protected from the weather. Ordinarily, these are located in underground chambers at the end of short side tunnels. Food may also be stored in crevices beneath rocks, in spaces around mounds of dead vegetation, and in cavities under fallen tree trunks. Mouthfuls of seeds, bundles of grassy stems, and the shoots of non-woody plants are all repeatedly hauled into these sites. Occasionally, pieces of the matter which is being transported fall from the wad between the lemming's jaws or get pulled out after catching on some snag along the side of a runway. This means pieces of weeds, fern stems and short sections of dried grass are frequently scattered along the tiny avenues leading to their underground caches.

Because of the vast amount of leafy matter that it eats, the bog lemming's droppings are far greener in color than the feces of any other similarly sized ro-dent. It is said that a person can determine whether the tiny runways through the brush or the entrance to an underground passage is being used by a bog lemming or some other type of mammal once a sample of the occupant's scat is found.

Like the lemmings of the arctic, bog lemmings experience periodic fluctua-tions in population, yet the swings in their numbers are far less drastic than those of their more northern relatives. During times of peak population densities, bog lemmings may resort to limited dispersal to other settings, but they never commit mass suicide by leaping off cliffs (and neither do arctic lemmings, as this popular myth has no basis in truth).

While most tunnels in the soil and, in winter, in the snow, are probably the work of voles, those seen in bogs, along the shores of peat-laden marshes, and in overgrown forest clearings and other cold, damp places may actually be occupied by the little-known and seldom-seen rodent that has relatives far to our north.

Plant Galls

In an attempt to remain hidden from predators and protected from the elements, insects typically select nooks and crannies in the most secluded or obscure places in which to pass the winter. A few bugs, however, hide in plain sight, as they spend this season within conspicuous deformities created on plants known as galls.

Galls serve as a year-round home to several types of flies in the gnat family and a few species of wasps and beetles. During the late spring or early summer, the adult fly deposits its eggs on the stem or twig of a particular type of vegetation. After hatching, the larvae burrow a short distance inward until they reach the center of the stem. The larvae then begin to secrete a chemical that closely resembles that plant's growth hormone. This results in an abnormal concentration of plant tissue around the larvae. As the season progresses, a noticeably swollen section of the stem or twig develops. Throughout the growing season, the fly larvae feed on nutrients that they take from the abundant mass of plant tissue which envelops them.

Research on the effects of a gall on a plant indicates that the tumor-like growth and enclosed larvae do not seem to significantly harm the plant's overall health. Plants that are afflicted with galls, such as stalks of goldenrod, may be slightly stunted, however, and do not produce quite as many seeds as neighboring plants without these parasitizing insects within their central stems.

Because many adult gall-forming insects do not travel long distances, eggs tend to all be laid within the confines of a relatively small section of land. Should a gall be seen on the stalk of one goldenrod, the chances are good that other similar tumors will occur on the central stems of other plants of that same species in the immediate area.

While these deformities can be quite conspicuous, especially during the winter after the surrounding vegetation has died, they are especially noticeable to several insects that have tied their lives to plant galls. One form of wasp is known to lay an egg inside an existing gall. Using a special, plant-piercing ovipositor, the wasp injects its embryo directly into the gall. When it hatches, the wasp larva kills and feeds on the immature flies. The wasp larvae are believed to utilize the nutrients contained in the tissue within the gall, much like the original fly larvae. With the end of the growing season and the death of the plant, the wasp larva enters into a dormant state, as would the gnat larva, and passes the winter within this visible chamber.

There are other insects that are attracted to galls, especially those that form at the end of a willow twig. Unlike the smooth-surfaced galls that form on goldenrod, the deformity created on some species of willows has a rough, irregular surface texture. The tiny crevices on the surfaces of these pine-cone-like structures are used by some specialized bugs for their homes, and by other small insects for food, as tiny bits and pieces from the mass of tissue can be picked off and consumed. Birds seek out galls, too: during the winter, the chickadee and downy woodpecker are known to peck their way into galls in order to reach the meaty morsels of invertebrate matter they contain.

A person traveling past a dried cluster of goldenrod in winter may note scattered deformities on the dead stems. It is possible to slice these open with a knife to expose the overwintering bug within this structure. It can be noted that some are harder than others. Plant researchers have discovered that the thickness and density of a gall depends on a complex interaction between the strength of the chemical agent produced by the invading fly, and the response of the individual plant to that chemical.

Eventually, in the spring, the occupants of this chamber return to an active state. They will gnaw a hole into the wall of the gall almost to the exterior. They then develop into pupae and finally transition into their adult stage and exit the gall through the hole made by the larvae. Following a brief breeding period, females will seek out the correct plants on which to lay their eggs to begin the cycle anew.

While goldenrod galls are the most common and easiest to spot, especially during this stark season, galls may be noticed on a variety of plants and in many locations. Each one is caused by a very specific type of parasitic organism. With a little luck, it is possible for the careful observer to spot one of these winter retreats, home to the few insects that have their residence out in the open.

233

Index

hummingbird 143, 155-157
june bug 98, 100, 130
kingfisher 100-103
lake trout 83-85
lateral line 85
lemmings 15,16, 228-230
mallard 124 -125
marten 11, 13, 45, 219-221
mice 6, 8, 9, 12, 13, 19, 20, 41, 42,
    45, 53-55, 118, 147, 151, 153,
    154, 161, 219, 229
milkweed 119-122, 139, 164
moles 7, 10-12, 99, 118, 152, 228,
    229
monarch butterfly 120, 162-165
moose 1-3
mosquitoes 55-57, 80, 100
muskrat 3-5, 8, 47, 128
nuthatches 28-30
osprey 97, 103-105, 160
otter 62-64, 97, 128
ovenbird 82-83
pheromones 111, 190
photoperiodism 10
pileated woodpecker 23-26
quaking aspen 40-41, 187, 196-199
ragweed 123, 140-141
raven 45, 99, 216-218
red-backed salamander 92-94
red squirrel 13, 19, 117, 143, 199,
    217, 219, 220
red-tailed hawk 160-161
reindeer 226-228
ribbon snake 138

shrews 9-11
small-mouth bass 131-133
snipe 69-71
snowy owl 15017
spiders 167-169,
starlings 49-50
swallows 79-81, 101
tamarack 187-189
tent caterpillar 146
tiger moth 144
timber rattlesnake 175-177
toad 7, 88-90, 117, 137, 171, 205
trillium 85-87
turkey 45, 209-211, 213
varying hare 12-13, 36, 41, 42, 42, 60-
    62, 148, 158, 198, 217,
    219, 224
vibrissa 10
voles 42, 45, 151-154
vulture 72-73
water strider 174-175
white pine 165-167
wild black cherry 146-149
woodchuck 177-179
woodcock 69, 71, 180-183
yellow-bellied sapsucker 141-144

Tom Kalinowski is an avid outdoor enthusiast who taught field biology and ecology at Saranac Lake High School for 33 years. He has written numerous articles relating to the natural history of the Adirondacks for various publications. Along with writing, he also spends time photographing wildlife. His pictures have appeared in various publications across the State. He occasionally gives lectures about Adirondack wildlife.

Sheri Amsel has been writing and illustrating natural history and science books for almost 20 years. Her newest work reaches educators through an online resource: www.exploringnature.org meant to enhance science instruction and help schools integrate outdoor education into classroom science. Sheri lives in the Champlain Valley in Upstate New York.

Your Adirondack Nature Notes

Your Adirondack Nature Notes

_____

_____

_____

_____

_____

_____

_____

_____

_____

_____

_____

_____

_____

_____

_____

_____

_____

_____

Your Adirondack Nature Notes

Your Adirondack Nature Notes

Your Adirondack Nature Notes

_____

_____

_____

_____

_____

_____

_____

_____

_____

_____

_____

_____

_____

_____

_____

_____

_____

_____

_____

_____

_____

Your Adirondack Nature Notes

Your Adirondack Nature Notes

Your Adirondack Nature Notes

_____

_____

_____

_____

_____

_____

_____

_____

_____

_____

_____

_____

_____

_____

_____

_____

_____

_____

_____

_____

_____

_____

Your Adirondack Nature Notes